MARIO OLIVERI

THE REPRESENTATIVES

The Real Nature and Function of Papal Legates

Preface: ✠ GIOVANNI Card. BENELLI

Postscript: ✠ SALVATORE Card. PAPPALARDO

VAN DUREN
GERRARDS CROSS 1981

DISTRIBUTED EXCLUSIVELY IN THE U.S.A. AND CANADA
BY THE WANDERER PRESS

First published with the approval of the ecclesiastical authority on 28 November 1980 by
Van Duren Publishers, Gerrards Cross, England.

Typesetting by Delworth, Colnbrook, Slough, Berkshire.

Cover design: James Gillison.

Library of Congress Catalog Card Number: 81-108272

ISBN 0-905715-20-9

Printed in the U.S.A. by the
Wanderer Press, 201 Ohio Street, St. Paul, Mn. 55107

THE REPRESENTATIVES

I DEDICATE THIS BOOK TO MY BELOVED PARENTS TO
WHOM I OWE EVERYTHING

on the occasion of their Golden Wedding

Published in the Diocese of Northampton

Nihil Obstat, 1980

Timothy Russ, M.A.,
Censor.

Imprimatur

+ CHARLES ALEXANDER GRANT
Bishop of Northampton

CONTENTS

NOTA BENE

It must be stressed that for a precise understanding of what is contained in this book, the reader who is not familiar with the Sacred Sciences ought to pay close attention not only to the significance of the abbreviations - this is obvious - but also and particularly to the proper and specific meaning of certain terms which are not always used in the same way as in a secular sphere. They must be interpreted within the context of the Church's Doctrine, and in particular of the Documents of the Second Vatican Council to which this work makes constant reference.

For example, the term *World* might be cited. The Council, in its Pastoral Constitution *Gaudium et Spes,* gives this definition: "The whole human family seen in the context of everything which envelopes it". Similarly *Ecclesiology* must be interpreted as "The Theological Science concerned with the nature of the Church", in so far as it is the Mystical Body of Christ, the Community of the followers of Christ, in its spiritual, social, hierarchical and ministerial Organization. This is not to be confused with the term when it signifies "the science of church building and decoration"! The same applies to the use of the adjectives *ecclesiological* and *ecclesial,* and there are many other examples that could be mentioned.

ACKNOWLEDGEMENTS

It gives me great pleasure to see the publication in English of a work of mine which aims at making better and more widely known the real nature of Papal Representation in the Church and in the World.

I have presented the Pontifical Representatives as they ought to be, and indeed as they actually are, as an important sign and instrument for the realization of the supreme pastoral activity of Peter's successor.

The whole purpose of this activity is that the *Communio Fidei, Sacramentorum et Disciplinae,* which must exist between the Church of Rome and all the Churches, should remain complete and undivided. This is absolutely necessary if the Local Churches want to constitute the One and Only Church of Christ.

At the beginning of this work, I want first to mention His Eminence Cardinal Giuseppe Siri, Archbishop of Genoa, whose whole life has been one of total dedication to the Church. This devotion has been especially expressed by a clarity and depth of theological reflection which would be difficult to equal. He has been an inspiration to me, leading me to consider my work and service for the Apostolic See within the context of a kind of Ecclesiology going far beyond an interpretation which is mainly sociological and worldly, one determined by changing fashion but which is, in fact, ephemeral and positively harmful in its effect, dependent - as it sometimes is - upon models taken from secular society. To Cardinal Siri is due the deepest love and esteem of a spiritual son.

I also wish to recall with filial affection the Right Reverend Mons. Giuseppe Dell'Omo, to whom I owe my priesthood and who was also responsible for sending me to serve in the Holy See's Representation.

To all those who have in any way contributed to this work, I wish to express my warmest and most sincere thanks. In particular, I want to thank their Eminences Cardinals Giovanni Benelli and Salvatore Pappalardo, Archbishops respectively of Florence and Palermo. They have done me the honour of providing the Preface and Postscript of this book, and in doing so they have greatly enhanced its value.

Cardinal Pappalardo was my mentor in the study of Pontifical Diplomacy during my time at the Pontifical Ecclesiastical Academy, which prepares candidates for the Service in the Holy See's Representation.

With regard to Cardinal Benelli, I had the good fortune to work under his guidance in the Secretariat of State during part of his period as *Sostituto,* when he was amongst the closest associates of the Holy Father.

I hope to be able to treasure all I have learned by being the witness - and in some way the helper of - his extraordinary and indefatigable work.

To both Cardinals my sincere gratitude, for many reasons.

After beginning my study of Papal Diplomacy with Cardinal Pappalardo, I continued under the academic tutorship of Monsignor Achille Silvestrini, now Titular Archbishop of Novaliciana and Secretary of the Council for the Public Affairs of the Church. He is well aware of my regard for him.

As always, there are many things that can only be learned through practice and not merely theory, and I learned much under the guidance of my first Head of Mission, His Excellency Mons. Giovanni Mariani, in the Pontifical Mission in Dakar, which at that time included the whole of French-speaking West Africa. During the last few years, my experience in the Holy See's Representation Service has been widened while working with His Excellency Archbishop Bruno B. Heim, to whom I am - in many respects - greatly indebted.

To both these Papal Legates I would like to express my warmest gratitude.

9

I consider it a blessing and a privilege to be serving at present in Great Britain at one of the most exciting periods in the history of the Church since the Reformation. Happily, after more than four centuries a new atmosphere is being created -and this too is greatly due to Archbishop Heim. I cannot but rejoice at the opportunity of being a participant in these events in a country whose people I have learned to love, and who will always have a privileged place of affection in my heart.

Special thanks are due to the Reverend Father Ronald Creighton-Jobe, of the London Oratory, who has been largely responsible for the translation of my work. He has accomplished this with exceptional skill, blending fidelity to the author's thought with the demands of the English language. I wish to mention with the same sentiments too Dr. H. P. Montague, who has helped to translate part of this work, and in this context, thanks must be given to Mr. G. D. W. Court, M.C., who has revised the text with a careful eye to detail. He has made valuable suggestions which have helped to free it from linguistic infelicities, particularly from Italianisms. I am deeply grateful to Mr. Colin Symthe who kindly gave me his expertise in compiling the Index.

Although I leave my Publishers, Mr. Peter Bander van Duren and his capable co-worker, Mr. Leslie Hayward to the end, my gratitude to them is heartfelt. I wish to say publicly how much I appreciate the enthusiasm with which Mr. Bander van Duren received the idea of the publication of this work; indeed, it could not have been greater had the book been his own. His enthusiasm and the skill which accompanied it have been remarkable, and not limited merely to the editorial context. It has been sustained throughout the venture, and without it this book would not have seen the light of day. To them both, my warmest friendship.

I welcome with much satisfaction the opportunity offered me by *The Wanderer* of making my book available to a wide readership in the United States of America and Canada, in a format that will be at once dignified and economical. The aim of my book will in this way be more fully realized, my intention being to make the true nature, and the theological basis, of the position and functions of Papal Legates in the life of the Church better known and understood. They are an actualization and extension to all the Churches of the special and unique mission of Peter's Successor.

I am therefore deeply grateful to the Publisher, Mr. Alphonse Matt.

It is my sincere wish that my book may help strengthen and deepen, in the United States and Canada as elsewhere, the conviction that the *Communio Fidei, Sacramentorum et Disciplinae,* which is absolutely vital, if all the Churches are to form the One and Unique Church of Christ, cannot be realized without "means of communion," without unifying realities. Among the visible realities, the ultimately unifying one is the Apostolic Petrine Ministry of the Bishop of Rome.

Such a determined conviction and practice - sometimes placed in jeopardy by certain currents of unrest and various disruptive ideas - cannot but further the faithful fulfillment of the supernatural mission of the Church, to which she is called, today as in the past, of leading all men to eternal salvation.

Mario Oliveri

28th January 1981
Feast of St. Thomas Aquinas

11

I welcome the publication of Monsignor Oliveri's work which deals with the real nature and function of Papal Legates. I am particularly happy that it is published in English, a language of straightforward communication, which is spoken all over the world. It provides a wide readership with accurate and concise information on a subject that is of great importance to the life of the Church. There is, unfortunately, widespread ignorance about this subject and also wilful indifference and misunderstanding.

The value of this work lies in that it gives, succinctly and lucidly, a careful and concrete analysis of the nature and function of Papal Representatives, that is based on sound doctrinal principles. These constitute in the context of the life of the Church an irreplaceable instrument for the realization of the supreme pastoral activity of Peter's successor, the Bishop of Rome. This is as true after the Second Vatican Council, as it has been throughout the whole history of the Church, though with different forms and emphases.

This work concentrates accurately on the dogmatic and juridical tenets of the Ecclesiology which emerges from the documents of the Second Vatican Council. Their interpretation is not inspired by sociological considerations but by the perennial, traditional doctrine of the Church. It is upon those tenets that the nature and function of Pontifical Representatives is based, and they are considered here in the context of *Communio,* (spiritual, social and juridical communion), of service and of presence.

Without wishing to comment in detail on the principal

ideas of this work by Monsignor Oliveri, and apart from any consideration of the great merits of the subject matter and its treatment, I should also like to strongly emphasize the pastoral value and importance of the mission of Pontifical Representatives, which is here repeatedly affirmed by the author. I do this, thinking of my own experience in the service of the Holy See's Representation as well as in the Secretariat of State - as *Sostituto* -, and on the basis of my present ministry as a Pastor of a Local Church.

This concept becomes fully acceptable if by 'pastoral' we mean, as we must, whatever has as its aim the attainment of the specific ends of the supernatural mission of the Church for the final realization of the Kingdom of God, towards which every activity of an ecclesial nature leads.

It is my fervent hope that Monsignor Oliveri's work, the result of his study and his priestly work in the field of Pontifical Representation, will be widely read, and so give to the reader a better understanding and appreciation of the real function of Pontifical Representatives in the life of the Church and in our society.

Florence, June 24, 1980 *P. Card. Benelli*

Giovanni Card. Benelli
Archbishop of Florence

INTRODUCTION

The aim of this study is to explore the position of Papal Representatives in the life of the Church today and in relation to its organic structure, bearing in mind what the Church in the Second Vatican Council says about itself and its relation to the World. The fundamental point of reference and the genesis for our thought, apart from the conciliar documents, will be the MOTU PROPRIO *Sollicitudo Omnium Ecclesiarum* (24.6.1969), which has as its subject the office of Papal Representatives (1).

When speaking of what an institution's position can be in the life of the Church today, it is very useful, if not essential, to consider what place it held in the past. There is a valid reason for doing this not only because the past clarifies the present (and this is true to some extent in every case), but above all because within the context of the Church the past often has a dogmatic force or a force of law which is normative in its relation to the present; as is the case in the sphere of Faith, or in that which pertains to the essential organic structure of the Church, as far as Christ willed it and the Apostles established it in its essentials (as for example the Sacramental and the ministerial, hierarchical structure).

There exist then, institutions which while not essential to the organic structure of the Church are, nevertheless, intimately related to it, and they are often based on Doctrinal principles as a foundation for their existence, to such an extent that the fact of their constant presence in the Church may itself be cited as proof of a Doctrinal principle.

15

It is necessary to state that the Organization and the Discipline of the Church could never exist apart from the foundations of Faith and Doctrine.

In the history of Papal Representatives, in order to place the question in its modern context, we shall limit ourselves to a summary of the conclusions of the first part of a much fuller work (2). We intend, therefore, to outline by way of synthesis some of the basic elements which underlie the primitive tradition of the practice of the Bishop of Rome in sending Legates to the Churches and of entrusting *suas vices (i)* to Bishops of particular Dioceses.

1.

As a basis for this one can say with certainty that from the very earliest days there has existed on the part of the Bishop of the Apostolic See of Peter a conviction, repeatedly and consistently expressed that he has a concern and responsibility for all the Churches. This is so because within the Communion which exists between the Churches that of Rome holds a particular and determinative position. This is true principally in matters of Faith, but also in fundamental Organization and Discipline (particularly when these are related to Faith). This concern and responsibility extended, too, to the keeping of the Sacred Canons, in order that the peace and tranquillity of the Churches should be safeguarded. Such a conviction was shared as well by the other Bishops who considered that the Bishop of the Apostolic (or First) See serves as the Guardian of the Faith and of the Sacred Canons established by the Fathers.

(i) the capacity to stand in his place and act for him;

2.

The most usual way in which the Bishop of Rome made his intentions, and in a sense his presence, felt in the Churches was to entrust *suas vices (i)* to others so that they might share in his Authority and position, and act in his name. These persons were sometimes entrusted with a permanent mission and were chosen from amongst the residential Bishops of certain important Sees *(Vicarii).* When they were sent on temporary missions to a Synod (or Council) or to the Churches, they were chosen from the Clergy of the Church of Rome or from the Bishops attached to the Roman Synod (Legati).

One cannot speak of a substantial difference between the one and the other because both acted as Representatives of the Bishop of the Apostolic See in those matters with which they were entrusted, and also as co-workers with him in the mission which he felt obliged to exercise with regard to all the Churches. The extent of their authority, the difference in the charge entrusted to each, the permanence or lack of it in their mission - all these do not appear to be very important elements in defining and describing the nature and character of their respective offices. Also when it became time the better to determine the different categories of Representatives of the Bishop of Rome [*Legati a latere (ii), Legati missi (iii), Legati nati (iv)*], by means of legislation and the teaching of the Canonists, it must again be said that at the heart of their mission there always remained the same essential elements.

(i) the capacity to stand in his place and act for him;
(ii) Legates sent from the side (of the Roman Pontiff);
(iii) Legates sent (by the Roman Pontiff);
(iv) Legates as such created by reason of their See;

3.

With regard to the charges entrusted to them, these were intended to make all Envoys share in the concern which the Bishop of Rome was held to exercise by reason of the special and unique place he has, from the mandate of Christ, within the context of the Communion of the Churches and their Pastors, as well as that of his own Church. This care and responsibility is, therefore, also a special one and in certain respects quite unique.

4.

The tasks which the *Vicarii* or *Legati* usually undertook aimed basically at safeguarding and fostering Faith and Discipline, so that the Faith remained intact in all the Churches in order that these might live in Communion and harmony with each other. To be more specific, their charges were concerned with the election of Bishops, the summoning of Synods, with establishing accord in controversies and in safeguarding the norms laid down by the Fathers or by the Apostolic See.

With regard to question of Faith their mandates extended solely to giving an account of the matter, or referring it to the Apostolic See. They never had authority to make decisions; the most they could do was to remove from Ecclesial Communion as many as did not hold the Faith defined by the Councils. Added to this, they had the responsibility of reconciling those who had given up heretical doctrines.

5

Moreover, the tasks given to Legates sent to Civil Authorities, whether these were on permanent or temporary missions, were concerned with matters of Faith or Discipline. They aimed at gaining from the Civil Authorities a proper co-operation (which, by the way, the latter felt duty-bound to give). This was particularly true in the case of the Civil Authorities in the East. These aims were by no means to be neglected by Legates accredited to the Civil Authorities as they came to develop in the West (when co-operation was required in summoning Synods or in consolidating the discipline of the clergy and laity).

The functions of these Legates acquired new dimensions, however, with the establishment of the Papal States, and with the affirmation of the Pope's Authority in temporal affairs. This is especially true when the Pope became the acknowledged Head of Christianity, and intervened as arbiter in the conflict amongst Princes and in the destiny of civil life in the West.

6.

With regard to historical and juridical development, in the process of change from one form of the legation to another, it would be possible to establish precisely defined periods only at the risk of oversimplification, which limits attention to certain aspects which are merely external and almost always marginal in their importance.

It would not correspond to the true facts of the matter to determine exact dates, starting from which the legations could be considered to be well-defined institutions, clearly established by law. It must not be forgotten that accepted practice and custom have always had the greatest importance in the life of the Church; nor is it essential for an institution's existence that it should have a precise code of precepts and norms.

7.

It would therefore be incorrect to think of the Nunciatures as definitely emerging from the end of the fifteenth century, as something quite distinct from preceding periods. In actual fact, particularly as a consequence of the Council of Trent, Nuncios had the same basic characteristics as Legates, with the addition of two others; the first of these was the permanence or established presence of their mission in a country, the second was their explicit assumption of responsibility in political affairs and their representation of the Head of the Papal States.

In fact, even before this, Legates had received commissions by which they were empowered to treat of matters which might be described as political, but then they had acted in this field as Representatives of the Head of Christendom. Now, however, in the political sphere they were the Envoys of the Sovereign of the Papal States. Christendom, conceived as the *Societas Populorum Christianorum (v),* was in the process of disintegrating and not all at the national States, which were being formed, recognized the position and the prerogatives of the Pope which he enjoyed with regard to the Christian world.

8.

The end of the temporal power of the Pope has determined the "depoliticization" of the Papal Representatives, and has marked the beginning of a progressive
(v) Society of the Christian Peoples, (or: Christendom);

20

"spiritualization" of their charges with regard to both the Church and the State, as was the case in the beginning (c.f. the Apocrisariate of Constantinople). Such a process of "spiritualization" does not imply a decrease in stature or effectiveness, but rather greater agreement with the basic nature of the Church. This has been complemented and assisted by the Second Vatican Council and post-conciliar legislation. How this is so will emerge from this present study.

PART 1

PONTIFICAL REPRESENTATIVES AND THE SECOND VATICAN COUNCIL

CHAPTER ONE

THE PROBLEM OF PONTIFICAL REPRESENTATIVES DURING AND AFTER THE SECOND VATICAN COUNCIL

THE ORIGIN: INTENTION AND STRUCTURE OF THE MOTU PROPRIO: SOLLICITUDO OMNIUM ECCLESIARUM

To present the question properly one has to keep in mind the uncertainty about the role of Papal Representation which developed during and after the Council, either from within the Council itself or from without.

The difficulty about Papal Representation arose largely from certain views of the Ecclesiology of Vatican II, and it is, therefore, in the light of a correct Ecclesiology that the discussion ought to begin. Discussion within the Council led to an expression of some concern about the matter, and the question posed prompted, in reply, the MOTU PROPRIO *Sollicitudo Omnium Ecclesiarum,* which deals with the office of the Representatives of the Roman Pontiff. The document revises and expresses more adequately the existing legislation and at the same time offers certain doctrinal principles which are useful as guidelines. The document encourages serious consideration of this whole question.

From an initial study of the MOTU PROPRIO, the need to consider the problem of Pontifical Envoys within the framework of Vatican II is clear. But the Ecclesiology which emerges from the Council should not be interpreted in a manner which is one-sided or biased.

I.

THE CONCILIAR DEBATE AND THE WISHES OF THE COUNCIL.

Particular interest was already shown in the Pope's Representatives in the document prepared by the antepreparatory Commission of the Council, and then afterwards in the interventions made in the Conciliar Assembly itself. The subject of Nuncios and Apostolic Delegates was touched upon in connection with the reform of the Roman Curia (3), within the context of the more general debate concerned with the relations between the Apostolic See and the Bishops.

During the forty-ninth General Congregation (October 16, 1963), Monsignor G. Amman intervened in the debate in the name of a number of Missionary Bishops. His intervention could be summarized in three points:-

a) Nunciatures present to the world a Church with a structure analogous to that of political power.

b) The duties of Nuncios could be entrusted to the Presidents of the Episcopal Conferences or to the Patriarchs. The advantage would be that these would have a deeper understanding of the language, culture and history of their respective countries as well as a better insight into the social, political and religious life in their territories.

c) The functions of Nuncios could also be entrusted to competent lay persons.

The Bishop began by asking whether the institution of the Apostolic Nunciatures should be considered as a tradition worthy of respect or rather as one of those wrinkles which appear upon the face of the Church, the shadows of which both John XXIII and Paul VI very much wanted to remove (4).

In the same General Congregation the difficulty arose of how the authority of the Bishops was to be reconciled with the presence of the Nuncios of the Holy See in Episcopal Conferences (5).

In the sixtieth General Congregation (November 5, 1963), Cardinal Gracias of Bombay made an intervention about the training necessary for Nuncios and Delegates. It should be essential for Nuncios and Apostolic Delegates, especially those sent to the East, to understand at least one oriental language. They ought to be prepared for their mission with an organized programme of study and lectures dealing with the history and culture of the countries to which they are going to be sent. Special emphasis ought to be laid upon philosophy as it is understood in Eastern Cultures (6).

In the sixty-second General Congregation (November 7, 1963), when the relations between the Bishops and the Roman Pontiff were being debated, the necessity was stressed of "... providing for the INTERNATIONALIZATION of the Curia and of making the Nunciatures conform to the needs of the age." (Bishop H. Van Der Burgt of Pontoniak, Indonesia), (7).

It was also stated that "many Council Fathers know by experience that they have always found pratical help in their difficulties, a spirit of understanding for their problems, and warm encouragement from the Roman Curia. This also applied to their relations with the Representatives of the Holy See abroad" (8).

The question of Nuncios was touched upon again when Episcopal Conferences were discussed in the sixty-seventh General Congregation (November 14, 1963). "Everyone clearly sees that Episcopal Conferences are useful. The scheme lays down that there should be a two-thirds majority within the Conference when matters relating to Civil Governments are in question. If, in these cases, there is no agreement and such a required majority is not reached, the entire matter ought to be given over to the Permanent Commission, or to the Nuncio or Apostolic Delegate so that there should be an established norm of Procedure" (9).

These interventions took place during the Second Session of the Council (1963) in the Conciliar debate of the *Schema decreti de Episcopis ac de dioecesium regimine (vi).* In the first *Schema* no mention was made of the Legates of the Roman Pontiff (10). This was also true of the second *Schema: De pastorali Episcoporum munere in Ecclesia (vii),* presented in the Assembly in the Third Session, and discussed in relations to new topics which were not already subjects for debate in the Council. But the anonymous report, which was edited along with the second *Schema* of the decree, affirms that in the *disceptatio (viii)* the Fathers of the Councils had submitted various proposals; among these was one which stated: *"In schemate agatur quoque de Legatis Summi Pontificis et de eorundem relationibus cum Episcopis" (ix),* (11). The report added, however:*"Nihil in novo textu explicite dicitur de Legatis Summi Pontificis ... quia proprium non est Concilii Oecumenici de quaestionibus particularibus agere" (x),* (12).

(vi)   Draft of the Decree concerning the Bishops and the Government of Dioceses;

(vii)   The pastoral office of Bishops in the Church;

(viii)   Discussion;

(ix)   The draft (or: the project) should also deal with the Legates of the Roman Pontiff and their relations with the Bishops;

(x)   In the new text there is no mention of the Legates of the Roman Pontiff ... for it is not appropriate for an Ecumenical Council to deal with particular questions;

In the voting held on November 4, 1964, there was a considerable number of votes *iuxta modum (xi)* and many of the Fathers were undoubtedly asking that the *votum (xii)* concerning the Legates should be introduced into the decree. In fact, in the Fourth Session (1965), the person responsible for the report, Archbishop P.Veuillot of Paris, was to state: *"Petentibus non paucis Patribus, in num.9 in fine ... expresse nunc affirmatur, quod implicite iam in textu habebatur, exoptatam Curiae reformationem respicere etiam Nuntios et Delegatos Apostolicos. Quare adduntur verba: 'Exoptant pariter ut, ratione habita muneris pastoralis Episcoporum proprii, Legatorum Romani Pontificis officium pressius determinetur'. Similiter in num. 10, (initio) ... expressa mentio fit de iisdem Legatis, cum post verba 'Officiales et Consultores' addantur haec alia, 'necnon Legati Romani Pontificis' "(xiii), (13).*

(xi) yes, with some qualification; or: yes, but subject to some qualifications expressed; or: yes, if something which is suggested is changed;
(xii) Wish, desire, desiderata;
(xiii) According to the petition of many Fathers, at the end of no.9, it is now said explicitly what was already implicitly contained in the text, namely that the Reform of the Roman Curia, which is greatly desired, should concern (or: include) also the Nuncios and the Apostolic Delegates. For this, the following words are added: 'The Fathers also greatly wish that in consideration of the pastoral ministry of Bishops, the office of the Legates of the Roman Pontiff should be more exactly defined.' In a similar way in no.10, at the beginning, there is an explicit mention of the Legates, when after the words 'Officials and Advisers' these others are added: 'and also the Legates of the Roman Pontiff'.

In the end, the Decree *Christus Dominus* contains three passages which concern the Legates. The Fathers say that "in consideration of the pastoral ministry of Bishops, the office of the Legates of the Roman Pontiff should be more exactly defined"(14), and that "the Legates of the Roman Pontiff should be chosen, as far as possible, from the different regions of the Church"(15).

Then, in speaking of the members of the Episcopal Conferences, the Decree states that in view of the special role which they play in a country, the Legates of the Roman Pontiff are not to be members of the Conference by right(16).

The Apostolic Constitution *Regimini Ecclesiae Universae,* (August 15,1967), concerned with the reform of the Roman Curia, which came into force as from March 1, 1968, deals only indirectly with the Legates of the Apostolic See in the sense that it assigns the task of dealing with them to the Papal Secretariat of State and to the Council for Public Affairs of the Church (17).

II

THE PREPARATION OF THE DOCUMENT CONCERNING

THE REPRESENTATIVES OF THE ROMAN PONTIFF.

The preparation of the document was, in fact, carried out in various stages over a rather extended period of time, as was necessary in the case of such a document which was directive and normative in character, and thus of considerable importance.

30

It is obvious that the opinions and the practical experience of Pontifical Representatives had to be kept in mind, and experts in the law had to be consulted. The opinions and the practice of the Congregations most directly concerned were also of great interest. The intricacy of this task can be seen in the formulation of the document which had to undergo various redraftings of subject matter. This was due, too, to a concern to present the right perspective.

The document was published on June 24, 1969, in the form of an Apostolic Letter, given as MOTU PROPRIO (18).

III

THE STRUCTURE OF THE DOCUMENT AND FIRST

IMPRESSIONS

The MOTU PROPRIO *Sollicitudo Omnium Ecclesiarum* is part of the determined effort of the Holy See to implement the reforms proposed by the Council or those reforms for which the Council Fathers had at least expressed a desire (19). We have said earlier that the Fathers had indicated certain feelings and wishes about Papal Envoys. The Pope explicitly used the MOTU PROPRIO as a means of replying to the request formulated in the Decree *Christus Dominus:* "We now intend, therefore, to satisfy the legitimate expectations of our Brothers in the Episcopate about this matter by issuing a document concerned with our Representatives to the Local Churches and Governments in every part of the world" (20). The request of the Fathers naturally gave rise to legitimate expectations and this seemed quite understandable.

31

The teaching and new theological perspectives contained in the Dogmatic Constitution *Lumen Gentium,* which deals with the nature and purpose of the Church, the Episcopate, collegiality and the pastoral ministry of Bishops, have undoubtedly made it necessary to reconsider the role of Pontifical Legates within the context of the Church's life.

This must be done to bring into clearer focus the origin of this institution, its nature, objectives, usefulness and limitations. At the same time one must face the question which some have posed (during the Council, but even more so outside the Council and in the period following it), whether, in fact, any justification can be found for the very existence of an institution of this kind.

The MOTU PROPRIO *Sollicitudo Omnium Ecclesiarum* offers a basis for a development in thought and takes into account the rapid expansion in theology of which results occurred during and after the Council; indeed, this development was so rapid that, according to one author, there was "a genuine accelaration in the 'tempo' of theological discovery" (21).

According to Cardinal Suenens, *"la théologie du Vatican II invite à reprendre les choses par la racine en fonction de la finalité de ces deux fonctions (la fonction diplomatique et la fonction religieuse). Et cela commande une profonde restructuration", (xiv),* (22).

(xiv) "The Theology of Vatican II invites to consider again this problem at its roots, in view of the purpose of these two functions (the diplomatic function and the religious one). And this requires a deep re-organization".

Serious consideration of Doctrine is always necessary if one wants to decide upon a practical course of action to be followed in the Church (23).

This is, in fact, the way the Council proceeded. The documents of a Doctrinal nature are followed by Decrees as practical developments or applications of Doctrine. And so, for example, the Decree *Christus Dominus* can be generally considered as a practical development of the Doctrine contained in the third chapter of the Dogmatic Constitution *Lumen Gentium.* Actually, as far as this chapter is concerned, the Decree contains little that is doctrinally novel.

A   STRUCTURE OF THE MOTU PROPRIO

The method we have mentioned was also followed in the MOTU PROPRIO *Sollicitudo Omnium Ecclesiarum.* The second section, which is practical and legislative, (containing twelve articles, divided into paragraphs), is preceded by a Doctrinal section, in which the teaching of the conciliar documents is recalled. The practical decisions and instructions depend upon certain important principles established by the Council.

I.   The document begins by affirming the Pope's rightful care and service with regard to all the Churches. This requires that he should maintain a suitable presence throughout the world, and that he should be aware of conditions in the various Churches. *(Enchiridion Vaticanum* (EV n. 3537).

It goes on to speak of the Authority which the Pope exercises over the entire Church as one which is full, supreme, universal, ordinary and immediate. This belongs to him by reason of his special office which is:

a)   to be the lasting and visible foundation of the unity

both of the Bishops and the Faithful; consequently his most important role is one of "holding together, undivided, the College of Bishops";

b)   "to strengthen his own Brothers."

It alludes to the testimony of Matthew XVI, 18-19, concerning the founding of the Church and the power of the keys. It also refers to Luke XXII, 32 which gave Peter the mandate to "confirm his own brothers", but it does neglect the witness of John XXI, 15 :- Peter, the Universal Shepherd, (EV n.3538).

The document continues by affirming the care which the Pope has to exercise for the unity of Christians and also his missionary responsibility, (EV n.3539).

The necessary precondition for the Pope's exercise of his manifold mission is a profound relationship between the Pope and the Bishops, between the Bishop of the Church of Rome and the Local Churches with each of their Pastors.

The traditional means of implementing such a *Communio* are:
a)   correspondence;
b)   the *ad limina* visits of the Bishops;
c)   the sending of Papal Legates, whether they are established and permanent or extraordinary and temporary (EV n.3540).

An extraordinary means:

The voyages of the Pope (EV n. 3541).

New means of furthering *Communio* after the Council:
a)   the Synod of Bishops;

34

b)   Some Residential Bishops being co-opted as members of the Roman Curia (EV n. 3543).

The document states the need for a movement which is two-directional: first, that of the various Churches towards the Church of Rome; the second, that of the Church of Rome towards the other Churches (EV n. 3544).

The activities of the Pontifical Representatives is presented as one of service in relation to the authority of the Bishops, (the legitimate autonomy of the Churches is fully respected), (EV n. 3546).

II.   The document then goes on to deal with the diplomatic mission of Pontifical Representatives.

The document's basic orientation affirms the right *(capacitas)* of legation of the Roman Pontiff, basing this right on intrinsic ecclesial principles (his special mission), and also on extrinsic reasons (the development of secular events), (EV n. 3547).

What makes it possible for the Church and the State to meet together on the level of diplomatic activity? While ultimately they have a different order (both are *societas perfecta,* and independent), they are, nevertheless, both at the service of man, their common subject, (EV n. 3548).

This necessitates dialogue and agreement for the purpose of:
a)   mutual understanding and co-operation;
b)   the avoidance of conflict;
c)   common efforts to find peace and promote progress (mankind's great aspirations), (EV n.3549).

More specific aims are:

a)   to safeguard the freedom of the Church;

b)   to assure the State of the peaceful objectives of the Church and that these are to their mutual advantage;

c)   to offer society spiritual support to enable it to work for the common good of all its members.

Diplomatic representation is a means of realizing these ends (EV n. 3550).

Finally, it mentions the relations with the International Organisations (EV n. 3551).

B.   FIRST IMPRESSIONS ON THE MOTU PROPRIO

From this first brief consideration, it is obvious that the MOTU PROPRIO is placed within the context of Conciliar thought, both in its general conception and in its particular details. One may find in this document the wider orientation of the Dogmatic Constitution *Lumen Gentium* and the Pastoral Constitution *Gaudium et Spes*.

The respect which it shows for the rightful autonomy of the Bishops is invariable (24). The legitimate rights of the Eastern Churches are particularly kept in mind (25). Throughout, explicit importance is given to Episcopal Conferences (26). Authority is always seen in terms of service (27), and the conviction is always maintained that the Church is, by nature, essentially missionary (28). There is, too, a deep concern for the unity of Christians (29), and the serious problems which confront the entire world (30). It follows then that it would be quite wrong to view the document as an attempt to reassert 'centralization' or as trying to establish an increased vigilance by Rome over the Bishops, and in particular over the Episcopal Conferences (31).

36

The document's basic orientation is theological and pastoral, but this does not cause it to neglect essential juridical considerations. On analysis, one is left with the impression that it was prepared, taking as its point of departure, the existing norms of Canon Law, but with a due concern for future developments, "keeping in mind the pastoral ministry proper to Bishops". The role of Pontifical Representation must be in harmony with this.

Two basic convictions emerge from the MOTU PROPRIO:
1) that the Bishop of the Apostolic See has a particular function (which is, therefore, proper to him and unique) within the context of the *Communio* amongst the Churches, and with regard to all the other Bishops;

2) that the Representation of the Holy See is a valid means by which the Bishop of Rome may best exercise his 'office' as Pastor of the whole flock.

Moreover, it would be difficult to find a suitable substitute for it. However, the document does not intend to suggest that the means referred to above is absolutely essential to the basic nature of the Bishop of Rome's particular Office or that there could not be at any time an alternative to it.

The MOTU PROPRIO does not seem a defensive document, and this is reflected in a total absence of polemic, but it emerges rather as a positive and constructive affirmation.

It wishes to present the role of Pontifical Representatives in the most positive light. It shows the Nuncio or Apostolic Delegate to be, essentially, a concerned intermediary between the Apostolic See and the Pastors of the Local Churches and their Faithful. The activity of the Representatives should be entirely orientated towards service. Envoys should cooperate in the Pope's name, in solving the great problems of peace, justice, progress and the development of peoples. They should help to foster the most profound ecclesial aspirations and those common to all mankind.

From the very start one can see that the justification for the existence of the Representatives of the Holy See is based upon the special position of the Bishop of Rome in the *Communio* of all the Churches. There is an intimate bond between them and the Primacy, of which they are a real and proper expression. The justification for the activity of these Envoys depends upon and takes strength from the extent to which their function emanates from and projects the supreme pastoral activity of the Bishop of Rome in the Church.

The Legate acts as the Representative of the Apostolic See in so far as it is the organ of the Universal Church. The Representative's function invests him with the basic character of one who serves in the Church and in the Civil Community. He ought to be a binding force, a link, a principle of unity, and a sign of the Church's universality. This involves two dimensions: that of charity, and the juridical dimension, which exists for the service of *Communio* in mutual love, in so far as it is a visible link between the Bishop of Rome and the other Bishops. This bond exists for the sake of creating, maintaining and increasing a unity which is called upon to be ever more authentic.

Finally, it is, nevertheless, worth noting that the Doctrinal section of the MOTU PROPRIO does not - in our view - sufficiently stress the *Communio* of the people of God and the *Communio* of all the Churches, nor perhaps does it draw out all the implications that the concept of 'collegiality' could offer. Using this concept as a starting point, one should be able to insist upon the necessity of the presence of the Bishop of Rome and his activity within the 'College'.

The 'College' of Bishops cannot exist or act if the Head is not present and active within it. The presence and activity of the Pope in the 'College' is also realized through the Apostolic Representatives, at least when the members of the 'College' are dispersed throughout the world.

CHAPTER TWO

THE PONTIFICAL REPRESENTATIVES IN THE CONTEXT OF THE ECCLESIOLOGY OF THE SECOND VATICAN COUNCIL.

Every Office within the Church must be in harmony with its nature, and it must be able, by its very constitution, to contribute as effectively as possible to the realization of its final end. One should be able to ask whether, within the Church, as it has been reflected upon and presented by the Vatican Council, a place may be found for the exercise of the Office of the Bishop of Rome in so far as he maintains a permanent presence, through his Envoys, in the Local Churches (32).

The evidence points to the fact that the Council has stressed certain characteristics of the Church which previously had not received such full consideration.

In his inaugural address at the Second Session of the Council, Pope Paul VI, expressing a conviction that was very widely shared by the Fathers, exhorted them to consider seriously their understanding and consciousness of the nature of the Church, because "there is undoubtedly a desire and a need to provide for the Church a more deeply considered definition" (33).

The Church has grown in self-understanding in the twenty centuries of its history, and the complexity of its life has expressed itself in a variety of ways without exhausting its richness (34). This should not be surprising since "the Church is a Mystery, a reality filled with a Divine Presence, and therefore, always capable of being explored afresh and in a more profound way" (35).

With Vatican II, the Church, assembled in Council, has given serious thought to its own nature, and has expressed this in an authoritative declaration. New aspects of its complex reality have been fittingly expressed and this has, without doubt, made possible a deeper understanding of the full reality of the Church's nature.

One can say that the characteristics of the Church stressed by the Council have rightly emphasized the primacy of the interior, invisible, spiritual and charismatic reality over that which is external, visible, temporal, social and juridical.

The priority in the life of the Church of that which pertains to its final end, to whatever is to be eternal, has gained a greater prominence than those things which are only a means to an end, merely instrumental in character. These last are destined to be utterly dissolved with the definitive Coming of God's Kingdom (36).

In the definition of the Church the concept of *mystery* is the over-riding one rather than that of *institution.* Similarly, the *spiritual* aspect prevails over the *institutional.*

The Conciliar documents intend to present the Church in a Trinitarian dimension (the Church as the fruit of the mutual labour of the Holy Trinity) - a realization of the saving work of God Who is One in Three Persons. It tries to place it in a Christological context (the Church as the fullness of Christ, the Body of Christ, His Kingdom and Family). Nor does it neglect the spiritual and charismatic dimension (the Church as a *Communio* of life in the Spirit; a community called together by Him, unified, enlightened and guided by the Spirit which lives and works in Him).

Reference is consistently made to biblical concepts and categories rather than to those which are social or juridical. The Church is, therefore, considered pre-eminently as a Mystery(37), a supernatural event which is both transcendent and salvific. It is viewed as "the People of God" (38), established by Christ through a living *Communio* of love and truth (39), a "Community of Faith, Hope and Charity" (40), a community whose end is salvation, the fruit of the work of Christ (its dimension of Communio).

The Church is also presented as a Sacrament in Christ (41), a universal Sacrament of salvation (42). Thus not only is it a "community of salvation", but also a means and an instrument of salvation, - "an institution of salvation" (its sacramental and ministerial dimension). And finally the Church is examined as a visible and juridical society (its social and juridical dimension).

While this last aspect was given a revised dimension by the Second Vatican Council (43), and assigned a more proper perspective, it cannot be forgotten that it is, nevertheless, essential to the nature of the Church in its earthly reality.

If in the passage of time, considerations which are historically conditioned, and therefore not essential, have caused one aspect to be given an exaggerated importance, one ought not to react by falling into the error of neglecting it altogether. The Church's various characteristics are complementary to each other. If one considers each of these separately, even though they may be true, they are, none-the-less, incomplete. They cannot be dissociated one from another. This is because "they form one complex reality which comes together from a human and divine element" (44).

Sound analysis of the documents of the Second Vatican Council can provide various texts which make it possible to form a correct evaluation of the social and juridical dimensions of the Church. It also enables one to see the proper meaning of the doctrine, evolved in the science of *Ius Publicum,* in which the Church is conceived as a *Societas Perfecta,* and why in the MOTU PROPRIO it is still described as such (45).

Actually, it must be admitted that an Ecclesiology which is too exclusively dependent upon the concept of 'society' may well have tended towards certain expressions of the Church's nature which were biased and one-sided, and which neglected other more fundamental aspects. The existence of the Church as a community constituted for and directed towards a union of life in Christ, through mutual love, may well have been a little forgotten, as well as the fact that the visible structure of the Church is quite *sui generis (xv)* in character (46). This may also have contributed to the idea that it could be reduced to a merely social and juridical entity (47).

In the course of time, the establishment of an Ecclesiology which largely tended to view the Church especially as a society and which was also too apologetic in tone, carried with it certain risks and deficiences. This, however, does not

(xv) specific; conform to its own nature; (or: of a special nature).

44

mean that it was a mistaken Ecclesiology, the main tenets of which are now unacceptable. It must be remembered that there would be other risks and gaps involved in a different sort of Ecclesiology which would neglect - or even hold in contempt - the juridical dimension of the Church (48).

It is in a Church, presented according to these insights, that a function and place must be found for the institution of Pontifical Representatives, in their relation to the Local Churches and the States. Therefore, in order to understand the nature and office of Pontifical Legates, it is proper to investigate all the essential characteristics of the Church, and the nature of its ministerial functions. To do this, it is necessary to keep in mind the documents of the Second Vatican Council.

Considering, then, that the Church is above all a *Communio* (possessing external, social and juridical qualities), and a *Communio of Churches* as well, bearing in mind at the same time that the Pastors of these Churches have to act in union with each other and in a special way with the Bishop of Rome, it should not be difficult to examine the mutual relations of the Churches and their particular relationship with the Apostolic See.

In a context of this kind one ought to be able to grasp properly the demands which arise both from unity and universality, as well as the *munus* which is peculiar to the Bishop of St. Peter's See, in relation to the 'collegiality' of Bishops. While doing this, it is always essential to remember that the nature and function of the Pontifical Representation is intimately connected with the special mission which the Pope has in the Church as the Successor of Peter. Therefore this Representation must be considered amongst the institutions of the Church which assist this *Communio*.

45

It seems, moreover, that the diplomatic aspect of the mission of Papal Envoys is to be placed within the wider context of the relations between the Church and the World, those between the Church and the Political Community, and also those which the Church has with the International Community. This is, then, the proper context for speaking of the international juridical 'personality' of the Church.

In order to put forward the various arguments, one would need as many individual chapters. But if we are to limit ourselves to the demands of a work of this kind, we will have to present some of the considerations which summarize the conclusions from our study already cited, and which will form the introduction and basis for an analysis of the legislation by the MOTU PROPRIO *Sollicitudo Omnium Ecclesiarum,* which deals with Pontifical Representation.

It would be as well to mention that the principal objections made against the Representatives of the Holy See, particularly after the Second Vatican Council, are based upon an Ecclesiology which does not take into account, in a global sense, all the teaching of the Council.

It happens in this manner if one limits oneself to a one-sided interpretation of particular aspects, such as the autonomy of the Local Churches, from which it is assumed that it is the Local Hierarchy which is entitled to maintain relations between Church and State.

It happens in this manner if one limits oneself to the 'collegiality' in its wrong interpretation, or the principle of subsidiarity, etc.

As far as the diplomatic sphere is concerned, such a limited view would maintain the necessity for the Church, in

a spirit of badly interpreted service, to strip itself of an aspect which might place it in confrontation with the Powers of the World.

Such a one-sided interpretation holds that the Church ought to labour in the world solely by means of the witness of its members, and not through juridical institutions.

These appear to be the basic objections which developed during and most particularly after the Council (49).

PART II

THE MISSION OF PONTIFICAL REPRESENTATIVES

AFTER THE SECOND VATICAN COUNCIL

This second part of the study of Pontifical Representation aims to explain the aspects of the MOTU PROPRIO *Sollicitudo Omnium Ecclesiarum,* which are more specifically juridical in character and which regulate the mission of Pontifical Envoys after the Second Vatican Council.

First, however, we wish to make some general observations which will, we believe, help to place this institution within the context of the Ecclesiology which emerged from the Conciliar documents. This will also make it possible to answer, in a general manner, all the questions posed in the conclusion of Part One.

CHAPTER ONE

DOCTRINAL PRINCIPLES

The Conciliar documents, and in particular the Dogmatic Constitution *Lumen Gentium,* as well as the Decree *Christus Dominus,* assert that the one and unique Church of Christ is a 'Body of Churches', a *Communio* of Churches in which the Faith and the basic organic structure, which is linked with Faith, must be identical, (an identical Sacramental structure, the same Sacraments and a ministerial-hierarchical organization which is also identical). These Churches constitute a *COMMUNIO FIDEI, SACRAMENTORUM ET DISCIPLINAE,* as Tertullian expressed it in his famous declaration (50).

It is, then, within the *Communio* of Churches that takes place the particular role and the unique position of the Church of Rome and its Bishop.

There can be no doubt that the Pontiff's 'service' to the 'Communion of Churches', and therefore of their Pastors, is special and unique and not reducible to the care and concern which the other Bishops too, must have for the Universal Church; it can and sometimes must also assume an authoritative dimension.

The means by which he exercises his concern and service for the Churches can be varied. One of these, which is characterized by continuity, is the despatch of his established Representatives to the different Churches. They become co-workers with the Bishop of Rome in carrying out his particular mission with regard to the Body of all the Churches and their Pastors, and therefore of the whole Church of Christ, one and unique. The Papal Representatives might be called

*Coadiutores Romani Pontificis in exercitio peculiaris muneris
sui, scilicet totius Christi gregis Pastoris vicarii (xvi).*

In this context, the nature and functions of Pontifical
Representatives are not at all contradictory to the principle of
'collegiality', which must certainly be properly considered
within the perspective of the *Communio* of the Churches and
their Pastors; but this, by its nature, includes the particular
and unique role which the Bishop of Rome, the Successor of
the Apostle Peter, has in it. Therefore, one can say that the
Pontifical Legations are the sign and the means of realizing
the intimate bonds of *Communio* which link the Bishop of
the Apostolic See with the other members of the *Corpus
Episcoporum*. The Representatives are not, however, the
exclusive means.

They are visible symbols and means of formalizing the
need which each Church with its Pastor has to remain open
and sensitive to the life of all the others, and in particular to
the Church which presides over the *Communio,* the Church
of Rome, which itself is determinant and binding in matters
of Faith, Sacraments and fundamental Discipline, in so far as
all the Churches must have the same Faith as the Church of
Rome, the same Sacraments and the same fundamental
ministerial-hierarchical structure.

**Only the Bishop of Rome, being the Successor of Peter,
is the ultimate 'Guarantor' of the Teaching and the Will of
the Divine Founder and Master, and he cannot fail.**

Pontifical Representatives are the signs for the Local
Churches of the necessity of remaining open to the demands
of unity and universality.

(xvi) Co-operators of the Roman Pontiff in the exercise of his special
mission, which is one of 'Pastor Vicarious of the whole Flock of
Christ';

And it is also by reason of the special function which the Bishop of the See of Peter exercises with regard to the whole Church that he is able, through his Representatives, to enter into dialogue with the Civil Authorities which give guidance in the life of the Political Community within which the Church of Christ is present and labours. This dialogue also takes place in the juridical sphere, with a validity on the international plane.

This is because the Church, which is organized as a Society in this world, through its highest Authority, which is the Holy See, is able to act effectively and juridically in the International Community.

This dialogue, established at the level of the Authorities - and this is also necessary in a pluralistic and democratic State - , and often carried on in the diplomatic sphere, attempts to bring about a more effective understanding and collaboration between the Church and the Political Community, for the purpose of serving the very same people.

It is a witness to a reciprocal autonomy and independence, and it is intended to make more possible the freedom necessary for the Church in accomplishing its mission.

This dialogue is also a means of effecting the presence and work of the Church on the juridical level within the International Community.

The service which Pontifical Representatives perform with regard to the Political Community cannot, however, be described in any way in terms of political activity; even these are essentially religious, though this does not imply, in fact, that they have no juridical significance. Such activities ultimately find their proper place in the work which the Holy See pursues and develops *ad extra* in the service of the Churches and of their mission.

The Apostolic See does this in order to bear witness also on this level - namely the level of the Authorities - and often in the diplomatic sphere, to the fact that the Church, while essentially concerned with establishing the Kingdom of God in the World, cannot, because of this, neglect any of the aspects of human life. It must be alert to, and collaborate in, solving the great problems of mankind, realizing that it is its special mission not only to proclaim the Gospel and dispense the saving grace of Christ, but also to give life, in a Christian way, to the human society, in order to safeguard the transcendent quality of the human person and its fundamental rights: *instaurare omnia in Christo (xvii).*

This also helps to promote the idea that the mission of Pontifical Representatives accredited to Political Communities is a religious and ecclesial one, because it is part of the function proper to the Church. This is in harmony with its nature, and seeks a dialogue with the Word and with mankind's institutions. This mission can be described as a religious-ecclesial function *ad extra (xviii),* while the role of the Envoys with regard to the Local Churches may be called a religious-ecclesial function *ad intra (xix).*

Any ecclesiastical institution, whether its sphere of activity is within the Church itself or in the World, must work towards ends which are proper to the Church; and, moreover, they must serve whatever is basic to the Church

(xvii)   to renew everything in Christ;
(xviii) ad extra = outside the Church;
(xix)   ad intra = inside the Church;

and pertains to its ultimate ends. This is because the external institutions which form part of the Church are ordered towards that which constitutes the inner reality of the union of life in Christ, the *Communio* of Divine life.

If it were possible to pinpoint a need which was most certainly expressed in the Ecclesiology of the Second Vatican Council, it is precisely that the juridical structures, having an essential role to play in the life of the Pilgrim Church - an instrumental function, pertaining to the order of means, to a passing reality - , ought to express clearly the fact that their nature is to be of service to the interior *Communio* of Love and Grace. If this is not the case, they become useless. Structures can only be of value in so far as they serve the ends for which they exist. They are not ends in themselves.

Papal Diplomatic Missions are part of the framework of structures which work directly to serve the social *Communio*, in the ecclesiastical sphere, and which are directed toward the interior *Communio* of Love and Grace. It is towards this that they are definitely orientated, and for this that they labour. This is the case with all the organs and instruments of government which operate within the Church.

It is in such a perspective that Pontifical Representatives have their place in the life of the Church, and from this that their function acquires its full vitality.

Nuncios and Apostolic Delegates act as ministers to the Bishop of the Apostolic See. The term 'minister' expresses the subordinate character of their mission. They act in the name and with the authority of the Bishop of Rome, but it also means that they are not purely passive instruments. In fact, they contribute personally and vitally to the exercise of their functions, the fruit of which depends on the individual Representative and also upon how he conducts his mission as Representative of the Holy See.

CHAPTER TWO

LEGISLATION CONCERNING

PONTIFICAL REPRESENTATIVES

The legislation in force concerning Pontifical Representatives is contained in twelve articles which form the normative section of the MOTU PROPRIO *Sollicitudo Omnium Ecclesiarum* (June 24, 1969). Along with the legal norms which are established therein, it intends:

1) to place the functions of the Pontifical Representatives in a proper perspective, within the context of the organs or government of the Church;

2) to establish a set of norms about their office which will more adequately meet modern needs, bearing in mind the pastoral ministry proper to the Bishops;

3) to abrogate previous regulations which may be contrary to these, (51).

This is, therefore, a piece of legislation which re-defines *"de integro totam legis prioris materiam" (xx)*, in accordance with what is said in Canon 22 of the Code of Canon Law. Some commentators on the MOTU PROPRIO (52) believe that it makes some important 'modification' to Lib. II Tit. VII,Cap.V, (c.265-270: *"De Legatis Romani Pontificis"*), without, however, affecting the other canons which are concerned, to some extent, with Papal Envoys (53). Nevertheless, it would seem more proper to speak of an 'abrogation' of all the canons in that chapter, with the exception of

(xx) again (re-defines again) the whole matter of the previous law;

canons 266 and 267 - *(Legati 'a latere'* and *Legati 'ratione sedis')*. This is because the subject matter in these two canons is not dealt with in the MOTU PROPRIO, while on the other hand, the content of the other canons is totally reorganized and ámplified.

I

THE DEFINITION AND CLASSIFICATION OF

PONTIFICAL REPRESENTATIVES

The definition of a Pontifical Representative (Legatus Romani Pontificis) put forward in art.I,par.1(54),only refers to the legislation contained in the MOTU PROPRIO. The title of Pontifical Representative in the document signifies:

- an Ecclesiastic (or Cleric);
- usually endowed with episcopal dignity;
- designated by the Roman Pontiff;
- to represent the Roman Pontiff in a specific way in the various Nations and Regions in the world.

a) No particular theological principle seems to demand, strictly speaking, that such a position should be limited to an *Ecclesiastic* or member of the clerical state. Therefore, it could even be entrusted to a layman (55). In so far, in fact, as a Representative is concerned, he will not be obliged to carry out any tasks - even with regard to the Churches - , which would require Sacramental Ordination. Some tasks might. involve the exercise of jurisdictional authority, but the principle that only Clerics can exercise such powers is recognised to be simply a norm of ecclesiastical, not divine law, (Cf. C.J.C. can. 118) (56). At any rate, exceptions to this principle were laid down in legislation after Vatican II (57).

However, it remains true that *"Ordo ex Christi instit-utione clericos a laicis in Ecclesia distinguit ad fidelium regimen et cultus divini ministerium" (xxi)*, (58). Further-more: *"Sacerdos quidem ministeriali potestate sacra qua gaudet, populum sacerdotalem efformat ac regit, sacrificium eucharisticum in persona Christi conficit illudque nomine totius populi Deo offert " (xxii)*, (59). It follows from this that the *potestas* which is for the purpose not only *"sanct-ificandi sed etiam docendi et regendi" (xxiii)*, is, in the Church based essentially on Sacramental Ordination (60), and that no one can exercise a proper (not vicarious) pastoral authority if he has not been ordained (61).

In the theological sense of the term, only the Hierarchy has a *potestas* of its own: the Bishops, and one amongst them, the Bishop of Rome, who has a special *potestas* by reason of the expressed Will of Christ.

Nevertheless, in their exercise of the *munera et potestas,* the Bishops have co-workers, who are established as such by reason of Sacramental Ordination. A particular Church is entrusted to the pastoral care of the Bishop, assisted by his

(xxi)   The Sacrament of Orders separates (or: differentiates; or: makes essentially different) by Christ's institution, the Clerics from the lay people, for the governing of the faithful and for the ministry of the Divine Cult (or: Divine Worship);

(xxii) The ministerial Priest, by the sacred power that he has, forms and rules the priestly people; in the Person of Christ he effects the Eucharistic Sacrifice and offers it to God in the name of all the people;

(xxiii) of sanctifying, but also of teaching and governing;

'presbyterium' *Episcopo cum cooperatione presbyterii pasc-enda concreditur (xxiv)*, (62). Sacramental Ordination to the priesthood and the diaconate in itself constitutes men as 'co-workers' in the Episcopal Order, and it gives them this essential capacity. Of course, they are co-workers with the Bishop not only in the exercise of the *munus et potestas sanctif-icandi*, but also *docendi et regendi (ordinis et jurisdictionis)*.

Yet an essential distinction must be made: in the exercise of the *potestas sanctificandi*, the Bishops cannot have as their associates those who have not received Sacramental Ordin-ation, at least in the exercise of certain functions, the greatest of these being the celebration of the Eucharist.

Whereas with regard to the *potestas docendi et regendi*, there is undeniably a more considerable scope for the activity of laypeople as sharers in the work of the Bishops. But it is not at all clear why Bishops ought in a normal way to entrust the role of being co-operators in the actual pastoral function of the episcopal office to the laity when they have the possibility of turning to those who have been made such by their Sacra-mental Ordination (63).

"A secular quality or character is proper to laymen .... The laity, by their very vocation, seek the Kingdom of God in temporal affairs and by ordering them according to the plan of God," (64). This is by no means intended to deny that in so far as they are faithful, the laity are sharers in the priest-hood of Christ, "that the priesthood common to the faithful and the sacerdotal and hierarchical ministry are closely interrelated," (65). Nor does it deny the principle that the faithful are able to give their wholehearted co-operation and assistance to their pastors and teachers (66), and that as has

(xxiv)   (A Diocese is a section of the People of God entrusted) to a
          Bishop to be guided by him with the assistance of his Clergy;

60

already been said, they have the capacity to be deputed by the Hierarchy to exercise certain ecclesiastical functions for the furtherance of a spiritual end (67).

It is, however, intended that in entrusting ecclesiastical functions to them, making them co-operators in the *potestas gubernandi* proper to the Pastors of the Church, this is not part of the ordinary structure of the Church, but is, rather, extraordinary in character. Moreover, it is not possible to speak of the "right" of the laity in this context. In fact, the exercise of an ecclesiastical office, given to a lay person, is always, by its nature, in relation to the sacramental power of those in whose name he exercises the office.

Applying what has been said to the case of Pontifical Representatives (68), there is no reason why the Bishop of the Apostolic See should entrust the office of being his co-operator to the laity in the exercise of his pastoral supervision of the whole Church except in cases and situations which are historically extraordinary.

Nevertheless, if the Popes were not giving any power of jurisdiction to their Representatives but simply a ministry, they would still always be real co-operators in the pastoral government of the Bishop of Rome, in the sense outlined above. This will also become clear in the analysis of their individual functions which follows. Nor can one avoid the fact that diplomatic representation to the States finds its real and ultimate foundation and justification in the *munus et potestas gubernandi* which the Pope possesses in the Church.

The States should clearly understand that a Pontifical Mission does not represent the Vatican City State, but the Supreme Authority of the Catholic Church (69).

When the Pope sends a Representative to the States, this is included in his own pastoral care of the Church and its mission. This is the reason why the same Ecclesiastic, who usually is also a Bishop, represents the Pope to the Local Churches and Political Communities as well.

Moreover, from the very beginning the task of representing the Bishop of Rome was generally entrusted to Clerics. At certain periods in history the preference was for Deacons, perhaps not only for practical reasons but also because of their particular ecclesial function, having been ordained "for service".

It appears that, in the Middle Ages, Princes were designated Legates of the Apostolic See, as for example the King of Sicily and the King of Hungary (70). Wernz notes however: *"Profecto Romanus Pontifex de plenditudine suae potestatis laico committere potest officium Legationis cum vera iurisdictione. Quia commissio laici est res plane singularis et extraordinaria, ideoque factum huiusmodi delegationis concludentibus argumentis est demonstrandum"; (xxv)*, (71).

Particularly in the early stages of permanent Nunciatures, there were some lay Nuncios (72). It is, however, undoubtedly the fact that at that time, before the Council of Trent, the function of Nuncios was also, though not exclusively, political. They were, however, exceptions (73). The practice of the Church and of the Bishop of Rome of choosing his Legates from amongst Ecclesiastics can be said to be a consistent one, and one which has been inspired by motives which are not merely practical.

(xxv)   Surely, the Roman Pontiff by virtue of his full power can entrust a lay man with the office of legation with a real power of jurisdiction. Since, however, such a delegation to a lay person is something very special and extraordinary, it should therefore be proved by means of solid facts;

In recent times it is quite true that with the development of Governmental and Non Governmental International Organizations, the Holy See has begun to send lay Representatives; (the MOTU PROPRIO expressly states this in Article II, par.1, EV n. 3556). Is this perhaps because the ends which the Holy See is pursuing with regard to such Institutions, through its Delegates and Observers, are basically humanitarian in character and not of a specific religious and ecclesial nature?

Certainly the goals which these Organizations are seeking to achieve are not especially religious but are more generally humanitarian, with their sights fixed on the common good of people in this world. This, however, is not to say that the interest of the Church in the great human problems does not form a part of its mission, which cannot but be religious and not simply political, humanitarian or philanthropic.

Delegates and Observers do not have the right to act with regard to the Local Churches. But wherever they are called upon to represent the Holy See as the Supreme Authority of the Catholic Church, they can act only in conformity with the nature of the Church which is essentially religious and supernatural.

Father H. de Riedmatten has written: "The aim of the Representatives of the Holy See is not to intervene in every situation, but it is essential that they should, however, honour their mandate, that they should work industriously to promote the whole range of goals sought by the International Organizations (74)."

However, since it is also true that these Envoys represent a spititual Authority, (and here again de Riedmatten is our source), the international world which gravitates around these Organizations, "while willingly accepting the presence of lay advisers at the side of the Representative of the Holy See, expects in the first place, that the representation of the Holy See should be made up, at least partially, of priests. This is because the nature of the Holy See differs from that of the other States represented. If the participation of lay persons in the delegation of the Holy See is often useful, one cannot stress too much the importance of the priestly presence (75)". What the Holy See requires, in fact, from its Representatives is that, above all, they should be priests (76).

b) The article then states that Ecclesiastics who represent the Holy See are also usually endowed with episcopal dignity.

It was said earlier that on the establishment of permanent Nunciatures, before the Council of Trent, there were also lay Nuncios; nevertheless, this was exceptional. During the Pontificate of Paul III (Alexander Farnese, 1534-1549), permanent lay Nuncios were definitely suppressed. This happened because the movement for Reform within the Church, which was increasingly powerful, demanded that the intermediaries between Rome and the States should, in the first place, be Clerics. This principle, imposed quite clearly by the special needs of that particular epoch, was to become an established custom which the Curia would observe from then on (77).

At the same time it was felt necessary to increase the authority of the Nuncios, especially those outside Italy, to act as a counterbalance to the local high Clergy. This was made possible by conferring on them the highest ranks of the Catholic Hierarchy. And so the practice grew up of creating as Nuncios, particularly those sent "beyond the Alps", residential Bishops or Archbishops. This was in contrast, however, to the practice of the Reform which strongly supported the obligation of Bishops to reside in their Sees.

It was essential to find a solution to this problem and so by a tentative process of development, determined largely by expediency, there emerged a system, begun by Paul V (Camillo Borghese, 1605-1621), of creating Nuncios Archbishops or Patriarchs *in partibus (xxvi)*. (With Leo XIII, the title was changed more precisely to that of 'Titular Archbishop'.)

Economic considerations were influential in checking the development of a system of this kind, since titular Bishops, unlike residential ones, did not enjoy any revenues. At first it seemed preferable to nominate Nuncios from amongst residential Bishops from small Dioceses in order to lessen, as much as possible, the effects of non-residence. Alternatively, the choice was made from a Diocese near some great centre, so that there could be some surveillance for the Diocese which had been deprived of its Pastor. On the other hand, on occasion, a Nuncio would be appointed who was Bishop of an important Diocese. In this case, he would resign and the Diocese would receive a new Pastor. The Nuncio would, however, retain his title and also a portion of the revenues.

And so various expedients were tried, but in the end none proved satisfactory because in practice they depended upon a legal fiction and were, to some extent, contradictory to the principles of the Reform. This led to a system, begun by Paul V, which compensated the Nuncios for the loss in prestige involved in not being residential Bishops, by giving them a more exalted title in the Hierarchy - that of Archbishop or Patriarch (78).

(xxvi)   (the complete expression is: 'in partibus infidelium'): in the unchristianized Regions;

65

The custom of creating Nuncios Archbishops and then extending it to Apostolic Delegates (who were first instituted by Pope Gregory XVI), became subject to some exceptions near the end of the Pontificate of Pius XII, but in 1961 Pope John XXIII restored the traditional practice (79).

Having surveyed, then, the historical considerations which determined the start of such a custom, one can ask whether, in fact, there are any actual motives of convenience which make the continuance of such a practice praiseworthy.

Meanwhile, it should be noted in passing, that this is the first time that the legislation states expressly what the actual result of a certain practice was. Nevertheless, by using the term 'ordinariamente' *(plerumque), (xxvii),* the way is opened for possible eventual exceptions which, if and when they occur, should not be thought of as at all extraordinary.

It is a fact that Vatican II has affirmed that Episcopal Ordination, together with hierarchical communion, constitutes membership in the Episcopal Body (80), with all the consequences that follow from this. (The first consequence is that it creates the obligation of having a concern for the whole Church. The Bishop must exercise this in communion with all the other Bishops and in particular with the Bishop of Rome). There is no reality, on the institutional level, greater than the Episcopal Ordination, which can establish a bond of communion with the Bishop of Rome and the entire Episcopal Body.

This does not mean that Pontifical Representatives, who are Bishops, are authorized to exercise the mission to the Local Churches by reason of their Episcopal Ordination. The immediate source of their Mission is the delegation by the

xxvii   commonly;

Pope to act in the name and with the Authority of the Supreme Pastor of the whole Church. Nevertheless, Episcopal Ordination constitutes the highest possible institutional charism, capable of strengthening them in the exercise of their mission. It also makes them feel in Sacramental Communion with the Bishops for whom they carry out the tasks assigned to them (81).

It must be stressed that this is merely a considerable convenience, and it should also be borne in mind that from the history of the Legations (as has been noted earlier), we know that the Bishop of Rome was, in fact, represented not only by Bishops but also by Priests, and, especially at certain times, by Deacons and Subdeacons.

Finally, it should be remembered that Pontifical Representatives, according to an expression already used by Pope St. Leo the Great, are called to be sharers in the special care and concern of the Bishop of Rome for all the Churches. They could be described as "Coadjutor Bishops or Auxiliaries of the Bishop of Rome in the exercise of his supreme pastoral government of the whole Church".

In fact there is an apt expression of this in the Decree *Christus Dominus,* where it is stated that Coadjutor Bishops and Auxiliaries are called "to participate in the concern and care of the Diocesan Bishop" (82). It is precisely because of this that they are called "Coadjutors" or "Auxiliaries".

c) The third fundamental element, which is included in the definition of a Pontifical Representative, indicates the source from whom he receives his Mission: the Roman Pontiff.

The Legation is established by force of a pontifical act

and this is distinct from the appointment of the holder of the office (83). The *officium* of the Legate is (84) nothing less than a participation in the *munus pastorale (xxviii)* of the Bishop of Rome which takes on the dimension of a *participatio potestatis totius Christi gregis Pastoris (xxix)*.

This is certainly a case of an essentially vicarious function which has its foundation and raison d'etre in the *munus peculiare* of the Bishop of Rome with reference to all the Churches and to the whole Church. We believe, therefore, that it can be said that the Pontifical Legate cannot be described simply as a personal representative of the Pope, but rather as a Representative of the supreme *munus pastorale* which belongs to the Bishop of Rome within the Church. And with this we have already touched upon the last essential characteristic in the definition.

d) The *officium* received is essentially one of **representing the Supreme Pontiff, in a permanent manner, to the different Nations or Regions of the world.**

It has just been said that we are not dealing with merely a personal representation but rather an expression of the supreme pontifical *munus.* As far as this is concerned, the Latin expression *personam gerere (xxx)* does not pose a problem; the two aspects could be resolved by saying that the Pontifical Legate represents the person of the Pope in his mission as Pastor of the universal flock.

(xxviii) pastoral office;
(xxix) a share in his pastoral power (or: authority) over the whole Flock (or: Church) of Christ;
(xxx) to re-present;

The article expressly states that what is being dealt with is an established representation; since the description is valid only within the context of the legislation of the MOTU PROPRIO, it must be said that it does not touch upon the roles of temporary and extraordinary Representatives.

Finally, the term "Nations or Regions of the World" is used. "Region" signifies many "Nations", since sometimes the Legate's representation extends to a number of countries; the territory of his mission (what was called in the Law of Decretals a "Province"), is not always limited by the boundaries of one country.

Paragraph 2 of article I (EV n. 3554) contains the classification of Representatives who are appointed in ordinary circumstances.

The paragraph can be presented, schematically, as follows:

PONTIFICAL REPRESENTATIVES

a) with an official mission only to the Churches:
   APOSTOLIC DELEGATES;
b) with a mission to Local Churches and to States and Governments:
1) NUNCIOS (equivalent in international diplomatic law to Ambassadors; they enjoy the right of being deans of the diplomatic corps, or, more exactly, the right of precedence);
2) PRO-NUNCIOS (equivalent to Ambassadors but without the right of precedence);
3) INTERNUNCIOS (equivalent to Envoys or Ministers).

A distinction is made on the basis of the Representative's mission itself, and there is a further subdistinction based on international diplomatic law. Introducing the first distinction, the legislation deals with the Legations to the Local Churches, describing it as "religious and ecclesial in nature". It distinguishes from this the mission to States and Governments by qualifying the latter as "diplomatic". However, it is our firm view that one can and should consider the mission to States and Governments as religious and ecclesial in character, without it ceasing to be, nevertheless, truly diplomatic (in an analogous sense), and of a truly juridical nature as well (also in an analogous sense).

The fear of describing the mission to States and Governments as religious may derive from the erroneous tendency to think that 'religious' is somehow in contradiction of 'juridical'; and the fear of describing it as 'ecclesial' may stem from the false premise that an ecclesial action can only take place within the Church or be directly connected with the Sacramental sphere. If the terms have any meaning at all, it is not apparent why an action which is "of the Church", and of the whole Church, even if *ad extra* cannot be said to be 'ecclesial' in the true sense of the word.

The two legations or missions, are, therefore, alike in nature: religious-ecclesial, the one *ad intra*, the other *ad extra.* This is so, even if what they do and their manner of accomplishing it, are different, as are their immediate ends. However, they differ *secundum quid (xxxi).* Both the one and the other are participation in, and an expression of, the exercise of the mission of the Supreme Pastor and visible Head of the Catholic Church (85).

This becomes more evident from the MOTU PROPRIO where it is impossible to distinguish which functions apply exculsively to the Representatives who possess diplomatic rank. Still, this does not deny that they are able to carry out their duties with a new capacity which makes it possible for them to embody the presence of the Church and its Head in a manner and form which are not possible for Representatives who do not enjoy diplomatic status.

With regard to the subdistinction of Legates who also have a diplomatic function (86), it is necessary to refer to International Diplomatic Law, using as a point of reference article 14, paragraph 1. of VIENNA CONVENTION ON DIPLOMATIC RELATIONS (Vienna 1961), (87). In this

(xxxi)   in some aspects;

71

document Heads of Mission are divided into three categories:

a) **AMBASSADORS, NUNCIOS** and other Heads of Mission of equivalent rank (for example the High Commissioners of the Member States of the Commonwealth). These are accredited to the Head of State;

b) **ENVOYS, MINISTERS** and **INTER-NUNCIOS**; these are also accredited to the Head of State;

c) Permanent **CHARGES D'AFFAIRES** (with letters of accreditation, *en pied);* these are accredited to the Foreign Minister (88).

Paragraph 2 of the same article states that the distinction of classes has no relevance other than for the purpose of establishing precedence and other ceremonial norms; it has no bearing whatever on the juridical capacity proper to the three classes of Representatives for the exercise of their diplomatic functions (89).

The article specifically places Nuncios in the first category and Internuncios in the second, but it does not use the expression Pro-Nuncio, because such a juridical personage only appeared later, in 1965, with the nomination of two 'Apostolic Pro-Nuncios' in Kenya and Zambia (90).

In order to understand the significance of such a system of classification, reference should be made to article 16 of the VIENNA CONVENTION ON DIPLOMATIC RELATIONS, which determines the order of precedence of the Heads of Mission. After having established in paragraph 1 that the order of precedence within each category is determined on the basis of seniority of accreditation, paragraph 3 goes on to

72

state that such a regulation is not prejudicial "to any practice accepted by the receiving State regarding the precedence of the Representatives of the Holy See (91)".

As was the case in the REGULATION OF VIENNA, 1815, this is an exception to the rule of the objective criterion of precedence. Such an exception applies where, by the wishes of the receiving State, the Nuncio is always Dean of the Diplomatic Corps (even when he is not senior in order of appointment). Within the context of his own diplomatic category, there is nothing which would disallow an Inter-nuncio to be given precedence as well. However, he could not be Dean of the Diplomatic Corps at all, since by custom the position of Dean belongs to the most senior by accreditation in the higher category (92).

The custom, almost generally observed by the States, of entering into diplomatic relations on an ambassadorial level with the appointment of Representatives belonging to the first category, has encouraged the Holy See to seek a new formula for establishing Nunciatures and for accrediting Representatives of the first rank also to those States who do not wish to guarantee the right of precedence and the position of Dean of the Diplomatic Corps to the Envoy of the Holy See. It is for this reason that the position of APOSTOLIC PRO-NUNCIO has emerged (93).

The actual meaning of the title is different from that of the past, when it signified a Nuncio who had been created a Cardinal, for the time during which he continued to exercise his functions before being appointed to the Roman Curia (94). In a certain sense it continues to indicate that this is consider-ed a temporary situation, at least by the Holy See, in the hope of being able later to appoint a Nuncio, to whom recognition of the right of precedence will be given.

Such an attitude on the part of the Holy See is determined neither by ambition nor by any desire for dominance in the sphere of the International Community; it arises, rather, from the sincere wish that the members of that Community should recognise its particular nature, the completely unique function which the Church can exercise through the Holy See within the context of the International Community - that is to say, spiritual and moral inspiration in the international order (95). This desire is not inconsistent with the mission of service which the Church wishes to exercise, and should accomplish in the context of social institutions, whether in the national or supernational orders.

The Church, however, does not, in order that it might maintain a presence, refuse to accept for its diplomatic Representatives a position which is not fully in keeping with its nature and spiritual dignity. This presence is already a witness to transcendent religious and spiritual values. "A position of pre-eminence for the Holy See, in international assemblies", writes G. Olivero, "can make itself felt through its contribution in essential matters, in so far as, within the Organizations in which the Church intervenes through its Representatives, their serenity and objectivity in defending principles, in putting forward proposals detached from material interests and from earthly, partisan considerations, can and ought to acquire for the Holy See an effective leadership in the transaction of affairs".

Since the matter seems quite clear, there is no need to emphasize that this diversified presence of the Holy See in international life, relations and discussions belongs, properly, to the Holy See as the sovereign and supreme organ of the Catholic Church and not by reason of the modest, but nevertheless indispensable, tiny State of the Vatican City (96).

Paragraph 3 of article I (EV n. 3555) introduces the use

of a terminology which can be described as 'special', since while it indicates in the proper sense of the term a Pontifical Representative (who has, therefore, the characteristics set out in paragraph 1), nevertheless because of special circumstances of time or place, this Representative is given titles different from those which have been previously considered. There are the following categories:

a) APOSTOLIC DELEGATE AND ENVOY OF THE HOLY SEE TO A GOVERN—MENT. A Representative of the Holy See with this title was accredited to the Government of the Federal Socialist Republic of Yugoslavia on September 17, 1966. The *Annuario Pontificio* noted this in the list of Representatives who enjoy diplomatic status (97). Actually, it was the first case of representation by the Holy See to a European Socialist Government. This special position has ceased in Yugoslavia since the decision reached by the Holy See and the Federal Socialist Republic of Yugoslavia to arrive at an exchange of diplomatic representation with that of the Holy See possessing the rank of an Apostolic Nunciature and that of Yugoslavia having the standing of an Embassy (98).

The particular case of Yugoslavia could be repeated in the case of other Nations, and we think that this is the reason why such a category was included in the normative section of the MOTU PROPRIO.

b) **REGENT.** This appointment is one which has an established and stable character but is meant to be substitutive or supplementary. A Regent would be sent when there is a long absence of the Head of Mission of the first and second class (99).

c) **CHARGÉ D'AFFAIRES WITH LETTERS** *(Curam Agens ad Negotia publicis litteris instructus).* This category is also one which is established and normally supplementary in character. Article I, already quoted, of the VIENNA CONVENTION ON DIPLOMATIC RELATIONS states that a Chargé d'Affaires belongs to the third class of Heads of Mission and is accredited to the Minister for Foreign Affairs (100).

OTHER REPRESENTATIVES OF THE HOLY SEE

Article II (EV nn. 3556-3558) of the MOTU PROPRIO mentions briefly other categories of Representatives of the Holy See; those who carry out their mission neither to the Local Churches nor to the States but to the International Organizations, Conferences and Congresses. Then there are those who, although they exercise their mission both to the Local Churches and to the States, are nevertheless 'substitutes', provisional Representatives in the temporary vacancy or in the absence of a Head of Mission.

All these, although they effectively represent the Holy See in their mission *(personam gerunt Sanctae Sedis)*, are not included in the MOTU PROPRIO in the category of Pontifical Representatives, since they do not in some respects fully satisfy the requirements for such a designation according to the definition of article I, paragraph 1. Therefore, the norms established in the MOTU PROPRIO do not extend to them, unless they are specifically named (101).
They are:

a) **DELEGATES.** These can be Heads or Members of a Mission to an International Organization of which the Holy See is a member, or Heads or Members of a Mission of the Holy See, participating with voting rights in a Conference or International Congress (102).

b) **OBSERVERS.** These can be Heads or Members of a Mission to an International Body of which the Holy See is not a member, or Heads or Members of a Mission of the Holy See, participating without voting rights at a Conference or International Congress.

It should be noted that both can also be lay persons, and, in fact, some of them are. The title of Delegate or Observer applies not only to Heads of Mission but also to Members. The Holy See has Delegates and Observers both to Governmental International Organizations and also to those which are Non-Governmental.

The fact that the Holy See might send Delegates to some and Observers to others does not mean that the Apostolic See has the success of those of which it is not a member less at heart, nor is this the case in Conferences in which the Holy See does not possess the right to vote. On the contrary, in the most important Organizations which rule or, at least, contribute to determine the destiny of mankind the Church could, with rather more difficulty, intervene *de pleno jure (xxxii)*, in order not to face obligations and run risks inconsistent with its completely spiritual mission. One vote more, one *sic volo* more would not change the final outcome, but would only expose the Holy See to dangerous compromises (103).

It is not on the level of concrete programmes, nor on the technical level in this sphere that the Church can develop its mission.

c) CHARGÉS D'AFFAIRES AD INTER-IM. *(Curam agentes ad negotia ad interim).* These are the members of the Pontifical Representation who, in default or during the temporary absence of the Head of Mission are empowered to represent the Holy See and not just the Head of Mission. Their position is substitutive and provisional. Such Representatives assume their functions both to the Local Churches and to the Governments (104).

(xxxii)   with full right;

II

THE BASIS FOR THE MISSION OF A PONTIFICAL

REPRESENTATIVE

Its Beginning and Conclusion

Article III, paragraph 1 (EV n. 3559) essentially reiterates Canon 265 of the Code of Canon Law, adding specific mention of the legation *ad extra* (105).

It should be noted that the exercise of the right of legation ad intra is an absolute right and carries with it complete freedom and independence from every other authority whatsoever, with regard to nomination, assignment, transfer or recall. (In practice it forms part of the fuller right which the Holy See claims to possess in its relations with whomever it might freely communicate; whether it be with the Bishops or with the faithful throughout the world. For their part, Bishops and faithful have the right to enjoy full liberty of communication with the Holy See).

The right of legation *ad extra* is in fact a *facultas, capacitas,* and its exercise should develop in conformity with the International Law. Even the Church, in so far as it is a member of the International Community (to the extent that it is analogous by nature to the other members) contributes to the creation of International Law. The practice of acting in certain determined ways, according to the norms of International Law, does not prejudice the liberty of the Church. This is because it will never accede to any practice or norms which might, in the end, be in contradiction to the natural law, or oblige it to assume a stance contrary to its particular nature. On the other hand, the fundamental principles which regulate relations between the members of the International Community are governed by natural law [as for example, *pacta sunt servanda, (xxxiii),*]; it is clear, too, that the Church is itself subject to the natural law and should adhere to it. Moreover, it is its interpreter and guarantor.

With regard to International Diplomatic Law, the Holy See participated in the Conference of the United Nations concerned with diplomatic relations and immunity (Vienna, 1961), and officially ratified the decisions of the VIENNA CONVENTION ON DIPLOMATIC RELATIONS. The Holy See has, therefore, contributed to the establishment of these norms (though these codify, in a rather general way, norms which had existed already through force of custom), and has bound itself to observe them. The norms which regulate the nomination, sending, and recall of diplomats and which are referred to in the MOTU PROPRIO are contained in the first section of the decisions of the Vienna Convention (articles 2 -19).

It should be noted again that while legations *ad intra* have their origins in a unilateral act on the part of the Supreme Pontiff, legations *ad extra* cannot exist except through mutual consent (106).

The second paragraph of article III (EV n. 3560) repeats almost verbatim canon 268 of the Code of Canon Law, which is concerned with the cessation of a Pontifical Representative's mission.

Finally, the third paragraph of the same article (EV n. 3561) establishes that apart from any pontifical measure to the contrary, the norm of the general regulations of the Roman Curia which fixes cessation from office at the age of seventy five applies also to Pontifical Representatives. It is

(xxxiii) agreements must be kept (or: respected);

not a rule, however, which applies *ipso facto (xxxiv)*, merely
by reason of the person having reached the particular age.

III

FUNCTIONS OF PONTIFICAL REPRESENTATIVES

Articles IV - XI of the MOTU PROPRIO (EV nn. 3562-
3583) determine, quite comprehensively, the aims of the
mission of Papal Representatives (107), what their functions
are, and what duties they have; what, in practical terms, is the
work which they should accomplish in a wide variety of ways
in the name of the Holy See and with its authority.

It is possible to subdivide these duties in the following
way:

1) With reference to the Local Churches, (art.IV, 1; V;
VI; VII).
2) With reference to the Bishops, (art. VIII, 1).
3) With reference to the Episcopal Conference, (art.
VIII, 2).
4) With reference to the Religious Communities,
(art. IX).
5) With reference to non-Catholics and non-Christians,
(art. IV, 4).
6) With reference to the Political Community, (art. IV,
2, 3; X).
7) With reference to the International Organizations,
(art. XI).

(xxxiv) by the simple fact that something happens;

81

1. FUNCTIONS OF PONTIFICAL REPRESENTATIVES WITH REGARD TO THE LOCAL CHURCHES.

Article IV, paragraph 1: *"Praecipuum ac proprium munus Pontificii Legati est ut firmiora atque efficaciora in dies reddat unitatis vincula, quae inter Apostolicam Sedem et Ecclesias locales intercedunt," (xxxv).*

It would be of great value to examine the theological and ecclesiological implications of this paragraph. Here, however, we will limit our interests to bringing out some points of a more strictly juridical nature, in keeping with the purpose of the present section of this study.

The task *(munus)* of making closer and more effective the links between the Apostolic See and the Local Churches is described as *praecipuum et proprium* (108). And it is 'foremost' not only in the sense that it is the most important task, but above all because the other tasks, at least those which have to deal with the Local Churches, arise substantially from it, and it is in carrying out this main task that the Legate finds the greatest service that he can perform for the Local Churches, and, consequently for the One and Only Church of Christ.

The fact that it is called the 'proper, specific' function of the Representative does not mean that this is the only, exclusive channel of communication between the Church of Rome and the other Churches. It is obvious that those who first of all and normally have responsibility for, and are the guardians of, *Communio* between the Local Churches and the

(xxxv) The proper and specific office of the Pontifical Representative is to render even closer and more operative the ties that bind the Apostolic See and the Local Churches;

82

Church of Rome are the Bishops, who remain true Pastors of particular Churches, by Divine right, as long as they are in *Communio* with the Episcopal Body, and directly with the Successor of Peter. What it means in fact is that this function belongs to the nature of the office of Legate as Representative of the Bishop of Rome. It is vested in him in his capacity as Legate of the Bishop who presides over the *Communio* of all the Churches.

This function is set out in a particularly positive and dynamic form to render ever closer and more operative the bonds of Unity, and, therefore, not only to maintain them but to develop and strengthen them, bearing in mind that Communion within the Church and between the Churches has a dynamic as well as a static aspect and is always in a sense under construction; this makes of the Pontifical Representative a Minister of Communion between the Churches.

Much will depend on the prudence and discretion of the Representative, to find the best ways and means to carry out such a mission. One thing is certain, that he will be able to direct his efforts towards that end if he follows the guidelines laid down in the MOTU PROPRIO.

A   INFORMATION

The functions established by article V are, in fact, wider than could be described by the word information.

Paragraph 1 (109) defines as *ordinaria* the function of keeping the Holy See regularly informed. It is the only function which is expressly called 'ordinary', in the sense that it belongs to the Legate by right, for the very reason that he has been made a Legate; but it is not clear why it is the only one so described and not the others, which are stated in the

83

MOTU PROPRIO, and which are also inherent to the office of the Legate (110). For whereas the CODEX IURIS CANONICI speaks of *potestas ordinaria,*, creating uncertainty in the canonical interpretations, the MOTU PROPRIO has the expression *munus ordinarium,* and this is probably also because it no longer has the *advigilare debent* of Canon 267, paragraph 1,2. The canon intended vigilance over the state of the Church to be a means for giving information (111).

Even now it is still true that, to keep the Apostolic See informed, the Legate must be familiar with, fully understand, pay heed to, and take part in events and in the life of the Local Churches within his sphere of duty, that is to say where he carries out his functions in the name of the Bishop of Rome. That is consistent with the care and solicitude which he must display as a co-operator of the Pope, so that the Successor of St. Peter can be helped in evaluating what measures are to be taken for the benefit of all the Churches, and so that Unity may be brought about in diversity and catholicity.

The duty of keeping the Apostolic See informed is one of the most important; it is both official and of grave responsibility. The information of the Legate carries authority, is *fidedigna*; it is an element of the highest value, a contribution of great importance, to which the Holy See gives its attention so that it can make its own decisions.

Clearly this is not the only element to take into account, it is not the only way in which the Apostolic See comes to know the life of the Local Churches; there are other ways which are extremely important: written contact with the Bishops as well as direct personal contacts - which in the future can become more frequent as communication becomes easier, Residential Bishops appointed as members of the Congregations, Synod of Bishops, etc.

It is an important responsibility of the Pontifical Representative to ensure that his information is objective, timely and as full as possible.

His knowledge and information should embrace everything concerning the life of the Local Churches: the Faith, the customs, the discipline of the clergy, pastoral developments, the fulfilment of the rules laid down by the Holy See, the relations between Priests and Bishops, the Religious Orders, Catholic organizations and activities. Other matters of interest are events in the nation and in civil life, which touch upon or have a bearing on the life of the Church. - In short, everything in which the Apostolic See can take a reasonable interest, in so far as it is a means of exercising its mission in the Church and the World.

Paragraph 2 of article V (112) broadens the function of the Legate by making him the spokesman of the Local Churches in their relations with the Holy See and vice versa.

Such a function could become particularly useful in bringing about an ever greater understanding between Rome and the Local Churches, and in eliminating possible misunderstandings. However, with regard to the fact that the Pontifical Representative presents to the Apostolic See the 'vote', the wishes, advice and proposals of the Bishops, Clergy, Religious and Laity, it should be noted that they, particularly the Bishops, all retain complete liberty to communicate their proposals, opinions and possible complaints, directly to the Holy See. It should be borne in mind that the Holy See reserves the right to ask the Pontifical Representative to give his views on whatever has reached the Holy See direct.

It should be assumed that the Representative will take great pains to pass on accurately the opinions of others, and not his own interpretation, although he may normally add his own evaluation.

The interpretation which the Legate will give, to whomever it concerns, of the acts, documents, information and instructions of the Holy See, clearly has no binding force in law, but nevertheless an important and semi-official value, in making clearer the meaning of items which are not always evident in the text.

It, therefore, becomes essential that the Offices and Departments of the Roman Curia follow an established practice in their dealings with the Legates as is indicated in paragraph 3 of article V (113).

These bodies therefore should:

a) not omit to inform the Legate of all decisions reached (this is always the rule);

b) transmit them normally (*plerumque*) through the Legate to the proper correspondents (there may at times be reasons calling for direct transmission);

c) ask the Legate's opinion before taking decisions which concern the territory in which he pursues his mission (this practice also should always be followed) (114).

B APPOINTMENT OF BISHOPS AND OTHER ORDINARIES, AND OTHERS OF SIMILAR RANK.

The role of the Pontifical Representative in this matter and the mode of procedure to be followed are laid down in article VI of the MOTU PROPRIO (EV nn. 3570-3572). This must be completed by a document of the Council for the Public Affairs of the Church: *De promovendis ad Episcopatum in Ecclesia Latina (xxxvi)* -; cf. (115).

(xxxvi) Candidates (or : those who are to be promoted) to the Episcopate in the Latin Church;

In accordance with paragraph 1, it is his function "to institute the informative canonical processes on the candidates".

Once a *rosa* of candidates has been formed, (normally three, which is why the term *terna* of names is used), the Pontifical Representative will collect, according to the accepted practice, the required information which he will send to the appropriate Congregations (for the Bishops, for the Evangelization of Peoples, or for the Oriental Churches) or to the Council for the Public Affairs of the Church, when it is a question of countries which have a Concordat, expressing *coram domino (xxxvii)* his own opinion of and preference for the candidate considered most suitable for the post.

In this task, which is extremely delicate and full of potential consequences for the life of the Churches, it is obvious that the better the Pontifical Representative carries out his duties, the more easily he will avoid the danger of being guided by personal viewpoints or motives; having as his one purpose the aim of helping the Apostolic See to select those persons who, in the existing circumstances, are best suited for the governing and well-being of the Local Churches (114).

Paragraph 2 of the article defines how the Representative should set about preparing the process for gathering information:

a) he will avail himself freely and discreetly of the advice of Ecclesiastics (Bishops and Priests) and also of prudent lay persons. He will rely on those who are in a position to provide sincere and useful information, and they must guarantee secrecy;

(xxxvii) before God;

87

b) he will proceed according to the norms established by the Apostolic See on matters *de proponendis ad episcopale ministerium (xxxviii)* - (in which also the main qualities required of candidates are laid down), always bearing in mind the responsibility and competency of the Episcopal Conferences. This has been determined by the MOTU PROPRIO *Ecclesiae Sanctae* (115) and consists, in essence, of proposing to the Apostolic See the names of candidates deemed worthy of being promoted to episcopal office.

It goes without saying that the Pontifical Representative will prepare the *terna* of candidates by giving serious consideration to those names which are proposed by the Bishops assembled in Conference or in provincial meetings. Nevertheless, such a list is not binding in the sense that, in specific cases, he is entitled to propose as candidates additional names which are not actually on the list;

c) he will respect the legitimate privileges granted or acquired and all special procedures recognized by the Apostolic See. In England and Wales, for instance, the Chapter of Canons has the right to propose a *terna* of candidates, which has to be discussed by the Bishops of the Ecclesiastic Province as a body, under the presidency of the Metropolitan.

Civil Authorities may, for example, possess legitimate privileges based on Concordats or Conventions or some similar agreement, or even accepted by custom. Certainly the Holy See wishes them to be respected, but the Second Vatican Council, having expressed its opinion that the Civil Authority should no longer have rights or privileges of election, appointment, introduction or nomination to the Episcopal office, has strongly urged those Civil Authorities currently in

(xxxviii) Candidates (or: those who are to be proposed) to the episcopal office;

88

possession of such privileges to surrender them voluntarily, with prior agreement with the Holy See; the effect of this would be both to guarantee fully the freedom of the Church, and to promote more suitably and expeditiously the well-being of the faithful (116).

d) finally, paragraph 3, (article VI, EV n. 3572) in emphasizing that "the law now in force regarding the election of the Bishops in the Eastern-rite Churches (117) remains unchanged, as well as the practice of designating the candidates by ecclesiastical jurisdictions entrusted to Religious Communities and depending on the Sacred Congregation for the Evangelization of Peoples", is reminding the Pontifical Representative of his duty to respect their competency in those elections.

C ECCLESIASTICAL AREAS

Articles VII (118) establishes the jurisdiction and duties of the Representative in matters concerning the creation, division, and suppression of diocesan or provincial ecclesiastical areas.

It is his function:
a) to promote the study of such matters, even on his own initiative, when it is required.
b) to present to the Apostolic See the proposals of the Episcopal Conference, accompanied by his own opinions (119).

Obviously the Representative will respect the right of the Episcopal Conference to formulate opinions and proposals, as is stated in the Decree *Christus Dominus* (120) and the MOTU PROPRIO *Ecclesiae Sanctae* (121); he will respect as well the special practice and legislation of the Oriental Churches (122).

2. FUNCTIONS - DUTIES OF THE PONTIFICAL REPRESENTATIVE WITH REGARD TO THE BISHOPS.

Paragraph 1 of article VIII (123) expresses in a positive manner what the CODEX IURIS CANONICI, c. 269, paragraph 1 stated in a negative way concerning the relationship between the Legate and the Ordinaries of Dioceses. In practice, the presence of the Pontifical Representative should not only not hinder the free exercise of the jurisdiction of the Bishops in the area of their Churches of which they are the proper, normal and immediate Pastors, but he should help them in the practical exercise of the jurisdiction.

The activity of the Legate, while it should be an aid and support in the pastoral work of the Bishops, is not meant to replace it: none of the tasks of the Pontifical Representative affects directly the internal life of the individual Churches to which he is sent; current legislation does not contemplate any normal function of the Legate which will compete with the functions of the Bishops, as was the case in the legislation of the Decretals. In addition, the special faculties granted by the Holy See to the Papal Representatives might very well not be the same as those granted to Bishops (124), but really extraordinary and exclusive; in so far as they could be of great service to the Churches.

It seems clear by now that the Pontifical Representative does not really enjoy an ordinary power of jurisdiction in the strict sense (one could speak of 'ordinary functions' which belong to his office, that is to say, by virtue of the fact that he is a Legate), not having authority to issue laws or decrees, to confer benefices, posts or assignments, or to pronounce sentence (except, of course, in exceptional cases, by delegation, or by being specially commissioned - i.e. by power of delegated jurisdiction).

Therefore he will refrain from exerting any jurisdictional power whatever in the Local Church, and will avoid anything which could even give the impression of interfering in the proper functions of the Bishops, whom he will make it his duty to aid and counsel, supporting and safeguarding their authority, because he acts as the Representative of a Superior Authority which stands for the general well-being of all (125).

The Legate's manner of carrying out his mission will largely determine its success. It will be the more fruitful, the more welcome he is, rather than being feared, or considered unacceptable and unbearable. His task is to be the man whom people may meet, and with whom they can speak freely and find understanding.

M. Cabreros de Anta lists the activities of the Pontifical Legates in relation to the Local Churches, and more specifically in relation to the Bishops (activities which he describes as 'pastoral functions'), by means of a threefold principle (126), that is:
   a) non-interference;
   b) direction; (the author specified "al menos de asesoramiento, de impulso, y de ejecución) - (127);
   c) co-operation.

In such a plan the Pontifical Representative, although he is not a member of the Local Churches, becomes a participant in their life and he cannot consider himself as standing apart from them (128).

It seems to us therefore, that the fundamental reason why he is not separated from the life of the Local Churches is not because he can and should help the Bishops in their 'practical' pastoral activity; in that way he might either put himself in the position of being a simple working partner of the Bishops, as are the Priests working in the pastoral field of the Diocese,or aim at dictating the pastoral activity of Bishops. The first possibility would make meaningless the mission of the Pontifical Representative as such. The second possibility would override the autonomy of the Local Churches and result in great damage to the Churches themselves. It is rather because he makes present and in some way realizes the specific function which the Bishop of Rome should exercise in all the Churches: The mission of the Pontifical Legate is basically and intrinsically Pastoral because it is part of the mission which the Apostolic See carries out for the Communion and the Government of the One and Only Church of Christ.

3. THE POSITION OF THE PONTIFICAL REPRESENT-ATIVE WITH REGARD TO THE EPISCOPAL CONF-ERENCE.

Although Episcopal Conferences were already in existence, it was only with the Council that this institution acquired special importance, and became established in its definition, structure and function (129).

The MOTU PROPRIO *Ecclesiae Sanctae* (August, 6 1966), in detailing the application of what had been laid down by the Council, called for establishing the institution where it did not yet exist, and provided for drawing up the statutes to be examined by the Apostolic See (130).

In order to simplify the terms of the relevant statute for Episcopal Conferences, to be based on the principles laid down by the Council [among them is that which states: "... having regard to the special function which they exercise in the territory ... the Legates of the Roman Pontiff are not, by right, members of the Conference (131)], the Consistorial

Congregation prepared a 'basic statute' (132). Article 8 of this, referring to the Pontifical Legates, visualizes their presence at least at the first sitting of every general assembly. Participating at other sessions could take place either by special arrangement with the Apostolic See or by invitation of the Conference itself. In fact all the statutes of the various Conferences repeat - almost in identical words - article 8 of of the 'basic statute' prepared by the Congregation" (133).

Paragraph 2 of article VIII of the MOTU PROPRIO (EV n. 3575) defines the attitude and the position of the Legate with respect to the Episcopal Conference of the country in which he conducts his mission. Therefore:

a) the Legate should bear in mind the great importance of the Episcopal Conference in view of the functions laid down by the Council (134);

b) it is essential that he maintains frequent and close relations with it, by giving every possible help in order to make the progress of its work easier and more successful;

c) he is not a member of the Conference, but will take part in the opening session of all general assemblies, except that further participation at other sessions will be at the invitation of the Bishops themselves, or by an explicit mandate from the Apostolic See (the present disposition merely repeats article 8 of the 'basis statute', referred to above).

The presence of the Legate of the Bishop of Rome at the initial session, while it does not impede the independent progress of the work and discussions within the Assembly, is, in fact, a sign that decisions reached can only reflect the close links and great attention which individual Churches should maintain with the whole Church, since their life is to be preserved in harmony with the life of all.

d) The Legate will be informed, in adequate time, of the

questions which will be dealt with by the Conference;

e) at the end of the meeting he will receive a copy of the proceedings, in order to study them and to forward them to the Apostolic See. Obviously it will not be a question merely of a formal transmission, but by means of his comments it will serve to facilitate, for the Holy See, the understanding and evaluation of the proceedings and decisions of the Conference.

4. THE RELATIONSHIP OF THE PONTIFICAL REPRESENTATIVE WITH THE RELIGIOUS COMMUNITIES.

Article IX of the MOTU PROPRIO (EV nn. 3576-3579) states the position and function of the Pontifical Legate in relation to Religious Communities, bearing in mind the juridical nature of those who enjoy pontifical rights (135), given their special links with the Apostolic See. The article also stresses the wisdom of reinforcing the cohesion and internal unity of the various Religious Communities, and also of their participation and co-operation at both the national and international level (136).

Given these premises, both juridical and functional, paragraph 1 states that it is part of the function of the Pontifical Representative to be close (*adesse*) with advice and action (*consilio et opera*) to the Major Superiors (137), in the territory of his mission.

The advice and action of the Legate are designed:

a) to promote and consolidate the Conference of the Men and Women Religious (to support their planning, development and consolidation (138);

b) to co-ordinate their activities in the apostolate of education, and in those of relief and social work.

94

In the exercise of these functions the Legate should consider not only the guide lines of the Apostolic See but also of the local Episcopal Conference, because the promotion and co-ordination of all good works and apostolic activities "concerns the Apostolic See throughout the whole Church, the consecrated Pastors in individual Dioceses, the Patriarchal Synods, and the Episcopal Conferences in their territory", (139).

The MOTU PROPRIO, article IX, paragraph 2, specifically determines (in a ruling analogous to that referring to the Episcopal Conference) that the Pontifical Representative will be present at the initial session of the Conference of Men and Women Religious, and will also take part in those sessions of the Conference which, by agreement with the Major Superiors, require his presence. He should be informed, in good time, of the agenda for the day, and will receive a copy of the proceedings, to study and transmit to the appropriate Sacred Congregation.

Paragraph 3 establishes that "the vote of the Pontifical Representative, along with the Bishops concerned, is necessary when a Religious Congregation which has its Mother House in the territory of the said Pontifical Representative, seeks approval from the Holy See and the grant of pontifical rights." (In fact the grant of status of *religio iuris pontificii* is made as a result of approval by the so-called *decretun lausid* of the Apostolic See).

Paragraph 4 concludes the article, noting "the Pontifical Representative exercises the same functions as in paragraphs 1, 2, 3 in regard to Secular Institutes, applying to them whatever is relevant".

5. THE RELATIONS OF THE PONTIFICAL REPRESENTATIVE WITH NON-CATHOLICS AND NON-CHRISTIANS,

One of the activities of the Pontifical Legate, which is particularly appropriate to the Church's commitment after the Second Vatican Council, is that envisaged in paragraph 4 of article IV (EV n. 3565); this deals with the promotion of suitable contacts between the Catholic Church and other Christian Churches and Communities, and with encouraging cordial relations with non-Christian religions.

In this activity, it is explicitly stated that the Pontifical Representative is acting in his capacity as Envoy of the Supreme Pastor of souls, who has, in a special manner, the ultimate responsibility of re-uniting all Christians, and of working in order that the Message of Salvation of the Gospel be accepted by all.

The Legate will also act in accordance with the instructions of the relevant Offices and Secretariats of the Holy See, and in agreement with the Bishops of the territory, especially with the Patriarchs in Oriental jurisdiction.

6. THE FUNCTIONS OF THE PONTIFICAL REPRESENTATIVE IN REGARD TO THE POLITICAL COMMUNITY

Some of the functions envisaged in the MOTU PROPRIO in this regard, are dealt with in a general manner, and their application will greatly depend upon the prudence and discretion of the Representative; others, however, are more specified.

It is not quite correct to say that the MOTU PROPRIO does not deal with relations with the Civil Authority except in article X (140), since already in article IV (which constitutes the principal article of the rulings) there is specific mention of action to be followed in contacts with the Civil Authority by a Pontifical Representative, even outside the context of diplomacy (cf.paragraph 3). Moreover, his interest in the problems of peace, progress and collaboration between peoples (cf.paragraph 3) will be most often realized, though not exclusively, in his relations with those who direct the civil life of a country.

With this proviso, it can be said that the functions of the Pontifical Representative in dealing with the Political Community are described in article IV, paragraphs, 2,3, (EV nn.3563-3564) and in article X (EV nn. 3580-3581). His task therefore is:

1) to interpret the solicitude of the Roman Pontiff for the good of the country in which he exercises his mission (article IV,paragraph 2). Obviously this can be realized best by means of his contact with the Civil Authority, without, however, excluding direct dialogue with other people, where this is possible. The fact that his dialogue is first of all with those who are responsible for the life and conditions of the people, does not mean that " la voix des pauvres n'est pas entendue " (141). The power to evaluate and to suggest what can be useful to the needs of the poor, in a specific situation, is worth much more than publicised and demagogic statements or attitudes.

Sometimes it will be necessary for the Pontifical Representative to impress on the Civil Authority the consistently peaceful and practical intentions of the Church. He is to be regarded as the interpreter of the true meaning of certain initiatives or teachings of the Apostolic See, which in a particular country or set of circumstances might not be understood, or might even be misunderstood. He will, therefore, clearly and fully demonstrate the thinking and teaching of the Magisterium of the Church;

2) to concern himself especially and zealously with the problems of peace, of progress and co-operation between peoples, having in view the spiritual, moral and material welfare of the entire human family (article IV, paragraph 2).

Such a function is completely justified, since the mission of the Church embraces the whole man and all mankind. Often, in this study, it has been stated that the Church's interest in the great problems of the human community does belong, from certain points of view, to its specific mission (though it is not its competence and function to offer concrete and technical solutions);

3) to safeguard - in co-operation with the Bishops - the mission of the Church and the Holy See in his territory, in his dealings with the Civil Authority (article IV, paragraph 3).

It is really a matter of working to the end that the Church and the Holy See can accomplish their mission with real freedom, and of knowing how to intervene, in the most appropriate way, in cases where this freedom may be in danger. Wherever Agreements exist, the Legate will be careful to ensure that they are scrupulously observed.

Any action by the Pontifical Representative in favour of the freedom of the Church has a bearing also on the freedom of whatever other religious community exists in the country (and that for the very good reason that it is part of the Church's teaching that the State should guarantee religious freedom both individually and to a community); so he will work, in a positive way, to ensure that everyone enjoys true religious liberty, and that this is guaranteed under the law.

Wherever the freedom of the Church is restricted, the task of the Legate will be more complicated in order to ensure that the Church can at least exist and accomplish its mission in the essentials.

The MOTU PROPRIO states categorically that the task of safeguarding the mission of the Church and the Holy See belongs also to the Pontifical Representatives who do not have diplomatic capacity (142). So these also will ensure that friendly relations exist with the Civil Authority, in order that a useful dialogue may be established.

It further states that this function of guardianship should be carried out in complete harmony with the Bishops, who are primarily responsible for the life of their Churches, since they are the actual and immediate Pastors;

4) to cultivate relations between the Church and the State (article X, paragraph 1), "in order to establish, develop and reinforce mutual understanding, co-ordination and collaboration, and to forestall or heal disagreements which may develop, so as to achieve the great human hopes of peace between Nations, internal tranquility and the progress of each country" (143).

In more detail, and still in article X, it is stated that the Pontifical Representative " has the commitment, normal and peculiar to his office (*munus proprium ac peculiare*) to act in the name (*nomine et auctoritate*) of the Holy See, in order:

a) to promote and favour its relation with the Government of the Nation to which he is accredited (144);

b) to deal with questions concerning relations between Church and State;

c) to concern himself particularly with the stipulation of *modus vivendi*, of agreements and concordats, as well as conventions referring to questions within the sphere of public law ".

Paragraph 2 of article X affirms the practical value of the Pontifical Representative seeking the opinion and counsel of the Episcopate in pursuing negotiations and keeping it informed of their development; this he will do in the manner and to the extent that circumstances permit.

It might be pointed out that this legislation merely repeats the practice already adopted in such circumstances.

7. THE FUNCTIONS OF THE PONTIFICAL REPRESENT-ATIVE IN REGARD TO THE INTERNATIONAL ORGANIZATIONS

The functions envisaged by article XI, paragraph 1 (EV n.3582) are to be carried out by the Pontifical Representative when there is no Delegate or permanent Observer from the Holy See, at the International Organizations which are located in his territory.

In these circumstances, the Legate should " follow accurately the programmes prepared by International Organizations ", and more specifically:

a) " inform the Holy See regularly on the activity of these Organizations:

b) " facilitate, in agreement with the local Episcopate, understanding for a beneficial collaboration between the Church's programmes of assistance and education and the corresponding inter - governmental and non - governmental institutions.

c) " support and facilitate the activity of International Catholic Organizations ".

Paragraph 2 of article XI (EV n.3583) concerns the Delegates and Observers of the Holy See attached to International Organizations, not in order to determine their functions (145), but rather to state that their mission will be carried out in agreement (*consiliis initis*) with the Pontifical Representative of the Nation in which they find themselves.

This statement could raise problems of interpretation. Of course, it must not be taken to imply any dependence on their part upon the Pontifical Representative. It should, instead, be interpreted to mean that, since they are not Pontifical Representatives to the Local Churches of that territory, nor to the State, they should refrain from any action which even indirectly could interfere with the religious and civil life of that country. For that reason they will not fail to follow the opinions of the Pontifical Representative of the region.

To conclude what has been said about the many tasks which the Pontifical Representative should carry out in various areas, paragraph 5 of article IV (EV n.3566) should be borne in mind. This establishes the direct dependence of the Pontifical Representatives on the Cardinal Secretary of State and Prefect of the Council for the Public Affairs of the Church. In fact, it is under his guidance and instructions that the complex mission of the Pontifical Representative should be carried out. Moreover, it is to him that the Legate is immediately responsible in the execution of the mandate entrusted to him by the Supreme Pontiff, to whom, nevertheless, the Legate is ultimately responsible.

By virtue of this ruling, all Pontifical Representatives are subordinate to the Secretariat of State and Council for the Public Affairs of the Church, in accordance with their particular competencies.

The difficulty of defining their respective duties as laid down in the *Regimini Ecclesiae Universae* can be, at least partially, overcome by the fact that the Cardinal Secretary of State is at the same time Prefect of the Council for the Public Affairs of the Church.

IV

PRIVILEGES, RIGHTS AND NORMAL POWERS
OF THE PONTIFICAL REPRESENTATIVES

These are laid down by article XII (EV nn.3584 - 3488), which in paragraphs 3 and 4, in a slightly different form, restates canon 269, paragraphs 2 and 3 of the CODEX IURIS CANONICI; however, paragraphs 1,2 and 5 are new.

The privilege established by paragraph 1 directly concerns the See of the Pontifical Representation and indirectly its staffing; it deals with the privilege of exemption from the jurisdiction of the local Ordinary. This is completely consistent with the nature of the Representation, which is exclusively under the Authority of the Apostolic See.

Paragraph 2 deals with certain normal faculties which the Pontifical Representative can exercise only in the Oratory (146) of his Legation, and this always in accordance with the rules in force in the territory. When possible, he should keep the local ecclesiastical Authority informed.

The faculties are:

a) allowing priests to hear confessions;

102

b) carrying out normal priestly functions;

c) performing acts of worship and sacred ceremonies.

In accordance with paragraph 3, the Pontifical Representative can give his blessing to the people and carry out sacred functions in all the churches of the territory of his own Legation.

This regulation is slightly different from the analogous ruling of the CODEX IURIS CANONICI. In this case it is no longer specified whether the Pontifical Representative has or has not episcopal rank (147) and, moreover, it requires that the Legate will, when he can, inform the local Ordinary in advance, and this he will always do, even if the functions are not carried out in the Cathedral; it was only in this case that the CODEX IURIS CANONICI required the Licence (licentia) of the Ordinary.

The right of precedence for the Pontifical Representative is dealt with in paragraph 4.

Within the territory of his Legation he has the right of precedence over Archbishops and Bishops, but not over members of the Sacred College of Cardinals, nor over Patriarchs of the Oriental Churches (148), always providing that these are in their own territory or, if they are outside it they are celebrating according to their own right. In comparison with the analogous ruling of the CODEX IURIS CANONICI, it is worth noting that there is less emphasis on the specification *licet forte charactere episcopali careant (xxxix).*

(xxxix).   although they are perhaps without the episcopal character;

Moreover, in the CODEX IURIS CANONICI there was no mention of Patriarchs. The legislation in regard to Oriental Churches stated that the Legate had precedence in respect of the *Hierarchae*, but not the *Patriarchae*, provided that these were in their own territory and were celebrating in their own rite.

Whereas before, in order that the Patriarch should have precedence, both conditions should be satisfied, now only one is required.

Finally, paragraph 5 of article XII explains the meaning and at the same time the purpose of the rights and privileges which belong to the See and to the Person of the Pontifical Representative. Their significance derives from the fact that they are a sign of the nature of the Legation, and they are granted for this very reason in order to facilitate the development of the mission and the Pontifical Representative's ministerial service (149).

The very right of precedence, honoured in the Church from the earliest times, is important as a sign of the nature of the function of the Legate, and in this sense must be used: **The Pontifical Legate represents the Supreme Pastor of the whole Church.**

On the other hand, the Legate is urged to use his rights and privileges discreetly and prudently; it might be said that he should use them to the extent necessary to achieve the ends for which they have been granted.

We conclude this part of our study by listing in order the new features of the legislation of the MOTU PROPRIO, in comparison with the CODEX IURIS CANONICI.

Article I   : new;

Article II		: new;
Article III		: restates Canon 265, but refers particularly to the aspect of the Legation *ad extra*;
	Paragraph 2	: restates Canon 268, paragraphs 1 and 2;
	Paragraph 3	: new;
Article IV		: new;
Article V	Paragraph 1	: restates in a better form Canon 267, paragraphs 1 and 2;
	Paragraph 2	: new;
	Paragraph 3	: new;
Article VI		: new;
Article VII		: new;
Article VIII	Paragraph 1	: new for the most part; however, it takes in Canon 269, paragraph 1;
Article IX		: new;
Article X	Paragraph 1	: re-examines, expands and specifies Canon 267, paragraph 1, 1°
	Paragraph 2	: new;

Article XII Paragraphs 1,2,&5: new;

        Paragraph 3   : re-examines in a slightly different form Canon 269, paragraph 3;

        Paragraph 4   : re-states in a slightly different and expanded form Canon 269, paragraph 2.

Of Canons 265 - 270 of the CODEX IURIS CANONICI, nothing is changed in Canons 266, 270 and in Canon 267 paragraph 1, section 3, where it says: *Praeter has duas ordinarias potestates, alias plerumque facultates obtinent quae tamen sunt omnes delegatae (xl)*. This could *de jure condendo (xli)*, be rendered in this way: *Praeter munera et facultates ordinarias* (among the ordinary faculties being, for example, those envisaged in article XII, paragraph 2), *Legati Romani Pontificis alias plerumque facultates obtinent quae tamen sunt omnes delegatae (xlii)*, (150).

Those Canons of the CODEX IURIS CANONICI which are not included in Cap.V, tit. VII of Lib.II, and which concern the Legates of the Roman Pontiff, remain effective.

(xl) In addition to these two ordinary powers, they commonly receive other faculties, which are nevertheless all delegated;

(xli) in a new law to be laid down;

(xlii) In addition to their ordinary functions and faculties, the Legates of the Roman Pontiff commonly receive also other faculties, which are nevertheless all delegated.

PART III

CONCLUSION

CONCLUSION

In keeping with the aims stated at the beginning of this work, we are now in a position to summarise the fundamental assumptions which underly the practice, dating from the earliest times, of the Bishop of Rome sending Legates to the Churches and of entrusting his mandate to Bishops of particular Churches. We will not, however, deal with conclusions or comment on matters which can be arrived at by a strictly historical approach. We only wish to define the position held by Pontifical Representatives in the Church today.

One essential concept emerged from the first part of this study: the sending of Representatives of the Apostolic See has been consistently based on the reality of the *Communio* which exists between all the Churches and Pastors. This *Communio* is not only spiritual and charismatic but also social and juridical and in this *Communio* is a particular and clearly defined place due to the Bishop of the Church of Rome, the Successor of Peter.

During certain periods of history, it was his *potestas* to which was given a greater emphasis. But throughout the long history of the Church it has always been " the care, solicitude, special mission and concern " which the Bishop of the Apostolic See must have with regard to all the Churches and their Pastors, to which preference was given. This must always be seen within the context of their reciprocal *Communio* of Faith, Sacraments and Discipline.

Pontifical Legations are a means and a vehicle for enabling the Bishop of Rome's presence and functions to be realised within the Communion of all the Churches. It is this fundamental concept which gives to a Pontifical Representation a continuity and homogeneity in its diversified expression and in the manner of its actual realisation.

This basic assumption also helps in the understanding and appreciation of how Pontifical Legations can fully exercise their functions and take their rightful place in the contemporary Church where, after the Second Vatican Council, new and particular stress has been laid on some of the components which contribute to the Church's complex reality. This reality is at one and the same time human and divine, a Society structured with hierarchical organs, and the mystical Body of Christ, - a visible society and a spiritual community.

One of the Council's statements which is especially important and fruitful, even if expressed with a certain hesitancy, is concerned with the fact that the Church of Christ, One and Unique, is a "Body of Churches".

The Faith and fundamental structure of these Churches must be completely at one, involving an identical sacramental structure and identical structures of Ministry and Hierarchy.

It is essential that all the Churches form a *Communio Fidei, Sacramentorum et Disciplinae*. Within the *Communio* of Churches, the Church of Rome and its Bishop has a particular function and place. Its position is determining and binding in matters of Faith, Sacraments and fundamental Discipline, in so far as all other Churches must have the same Faith, the same Sacraments and the same essential ministerial-hierarchical structure.

The Bishop of the Church of Rome is the Successor of

St. Peter and therefore the ultimate Guarantor of the Teaching and the Will of the Divine Founder, and he cannot fail in this rôle.

Seen in the light of what we have stated before, the nature and rôle of Pontifical Representatives do not in any way conflict with the principle of "Collegiality", which must always and at any rate be viewed and considered in the context of the *Communio* of the Churches and their Bishops. Nor does the principle of "Collegiality" in the least exclude the unique rôle which Peter's Successor, the Bishop of Rome, has within this *Communio*.

It can be positively affirmed that Pontifical Legates are the outward signs and means of actualizing (though not the exclusive means) the bonds of communion between the Bishop of the Apostolic See and the other members of the Body of Bishops.

They are the signs of the need which every Church and its Pastor shares of remaining open and sensitive to the life of all the others and especially to the Church which presides over the *Communio* : the Church of Rome. They must remain open and sensitive to the necessity of unity and universality.

It is because of the special rôle which the Bishop of the Apostolic See has in the Church that he can, through his Representatives, enter into dialogue with the Civil Authorities which guide the life of the Political Community within which the Church of Christ exists and works.

Such a dialogue can rightly take place on the juridical and diplomatic level as well as in the international sphere. It enables agreements and collaboration between the Church and the Political Community to be more fruitful in serving the same people, and at the same time it bears testimony to their reciprocal autonomy and independence.

With regard to the Political Community, the functions of Pontifical Representatives cannot be defined as a political activity. Their functions are essentially religious in character and find their context in the activities of the Holy See *ad extra* in its service of the Churches and of the World. The activities of Pontifical Representatives also bear witness in this sphere to the fact that the Church, while primarily and essentially concerned with the establishment of God's Kingdom in the World, cannot on this account overlook any aspects of men's lives.

The Church must be attentive and collaborate in finding a solution to the major problems of mankind, but it must always bear in mind that it is its specific mission to proclaim the Gospel. The Church must spread abroad the redemptive Grace of Christ in order also to give life to Society and it must do this in a manner worthy of the Christian Faith. The Church must labour to safeguard the transcendent nature of man and man's fundamental rights. It is the Church's task to *" instaurare omnia in Christo "*.

It has been stressed that the mission of Pontifical Representatives to Political Communities is essentially a religious and ecclesial one since it forms part of the mission of the Church. It is in complete agreement and harmony with the nature of this mission that the Church seeks a dialogue with the World and Secular Institutions. This is the justification for defining it as a religious-ecclesial function *ad extra*, while the mission to the Churches is a religious-ecclesial function *ad intra*.

Every ecclesiastical institution, whether it carries out its work within the Church or outside it in the World, ought to be orientated to the goals of the Church itself. Moreover, these institutions must be of service to whatever is fundamental in the Church, and subordinated to its charismatic dimension (using this term in its fullest sense). They must be ordered towards those features of the Church's life which are interior and partake of the communion of the life in Christ, - the communion of Divine Life.

If it were possible to point out one need which clearly emerged from the Ecclesiology of the Second Vatican Council, it would be this: juridical structures, while having an essential role to play in the life of the Pilgrim Church, must, nevertheless, show unambiguously that their function is to be of service to the inner communion of love and grace. Juridical structures are no ends in themselves.

Pontifical Representation forms part of the structure within the Church, and it works directly to serve the social and juridical Communion between the Churches. But Pontifical Representation must be directed towards and subordinated to the union of love and grace (*Communio vitae divinae*). It is in order to further these aims that Pontifical Representatives should carry out their duties, as indeed ought all the governmental organs of the Church.

Seen in the light of the true ecclesiological foundation, Pontifical Representatives are an integral part of the Church's structure and part of the Church's life. Their role is an extremely fruitful one, and they act as Ministers of the Apostolic See. This title 'Minister' expresses the very nature of their mission. They perform their duties in the name of the Bishop of Rome and with his Authority, yet without being merely passive instruments. In fact, in the exercise of their office they make an important personal contribution, and the success of their mission greatly depends on this personal dimension.

POSTSCRIPT
by
His Eminence Salvatore Cardinal Pappalardo

In the aftermath of the Second Vatican Council it is appropriate to produce a study on the lines of previous excellent examples which would deal in detail and depth with the whole scope of the historical and doctrinal basis of an institution which, in the past and present has been a sign and instrument of the presence and pastoral activity of the Pope in the context of the Church and of Society.

Monsignor Oliveri's treatment of the topic is the answer to that need and to other requirements and expectations; it has been carried out in a systematic manner which meets all the demands. It meets the demands of those who require a text which provides immediate consultation and information, as well of those who wish to study individual topics concerning Pontifical Representation in detail and who therefore require such a thorough study which also gives access to sources and a wide selection of literature on the subject. In this connection, the personal approach of Monsignor Oliveri is especially valuable, particularly in the second part of the work in which he is committed to presenting the real nature and function of Papal Representatives on the basis of the most recent documentary evidence.

Special consideration is given to the Pontifical MOTU PROPRIO *Sollicitudo Omnium Ecclesiarum;* this is the document which brings together all the values, interpretations and the original purpose of Pontifical Representation and which places them in the framework of the Second Vatican Council. It presents Pontifical Representation as a useful principle and a means towards the realization of the 'communion' between the Bishop of Rome and the other Bishops.

Since the Church should be and wants to be represented in the World, to share its hopes and sorrows and to exercise, hopefully, a beneficial influence on its diverse social and political elements, the Pontifical Representation is seen as an active instrument in the plan of the International Community and of its various organisms.

Sincere congratulations are due to Monsignor Oliveri, at present in the Service of the Holy See's Representation in London, for the complete, clear and also technically accurate presentation of the mass of material. I also express my sincere wish that the fruit of this work, summarized in all its conclusions, will be a better understanding and appreciation of the true nature and of the real ends of the Representation of the Holy See.

+ Silvatore Card. Pappalardo

Palermo, Italy

Salvatore Cardinal Pappalardo

Archbishop of Palermo

ABBREVIATIONS

A.A.S., AAS	*Acta Apostolicae Sedis*
AA. VV.	Various Authors
Art., art.	Article
art. cit.	Article quoted above
A.S.S., ASS	*Acta Sanctae Sedis*
c., can., cc.	Canon (singular and plural)
Cap., cap.	*Caput*, chapter
Cf., cf.	*Confer*, consult, see
Denz. - S.	Denzinger-Schönmetzer, *Enchiridion Symbolorum*
EV, E.V.	*Enchiridion Vaticanum* (Conciliar and post-conciliar Documents)
f., ff.	following (singular and plural)
fasc.	*fasciculus*, bundle of letters;
Ibid., ibid.	*Ibidem*, in the same place
I.C.I.	Informations Catholiques Internationales
Lib., lib.	*Liber*, book
loc. cit.	*loco citato*, in the place quoted above
n., nn.	number (singular and plural)
O.N.U.	Organisation des Nations Unies, United Nations Organisation
Op.cit., op. cit.	*Opus citatum*, work quoted above
p., pp.	page (singular and plural)
Par., par.	paragraph
Tit., tit.	*Titulus*, title
Tom., t.	*Tomus*, tome, book
Vol., vol., voll.	Volume (singular and plural)

REFERENCES

1. Cf. *A.A.S.*, 61 (1969), pp. 473-484.

2. Cf. MARIO OLIVERI, *Natura e funzioni dei Legati Pontifici nella storia e nel contesto ecclesiologico del Vaticano II*, Marietti, Torino (1979), pp. 320.

3. Cf. I. GORDON, *De Curia Romana renovata, Renovatio 'desiderata' et renovatio 'facta' conferuntur*, in: Periodica, 58 (1969), p. 98 f.

4. Cf. Il *Concilio Vaticano II - Cronache del Concilio Vaticano II*, edited from *La Civiltà Cattolica*, under the direction of G. CAPRILE, Second Period 1963-1964, Vol. III, Roma (1966), p. 98, n.l.

5. Cf. Ibid., n.3.

6. Ibid., p. 189, n.3.

7. Ibid., p. 209, n.18

8. Ibid., p. 210, n.18.

9. Ibid., p. 269, n.10.

10. However, the Introduction to the report on the schema of the Decree 'de Episcopis ac de Dioecesium Regimine', read in the Assembly during the 60th General Congregation (Nov 5, 1963) by Cardinal Marella, mentions Nuncios and Apostolic Delegates. It explains that they are extremely useful in assisting the Holy See to understand the state of affairs in particular places as well as performing a service for the Bishops in the spiritual and

administrative oversight of their Dioceses.

'Per legatos enim Romani Pontificis faciliores et expeditiores fiunt Ordinariorum relationes cum Sede Apostolica, integro servato libero propriae eorum cuiusque iuridictionis exercitio (cf. C.I.C., can. 269, par.1). Nuntiis autem committitur praeterea ut, secundum normas a Sancta Sede receptas, relationes foveant inter Sedem Apostolicam et civilia Gubernia apud quae legatione stabili funguntur, ut iura Ecclesiae eiusdemque libertas et autonomia tutentur ad bonum fidelium melius et efficacius promovendum: quod, profecto, etiam in magnum commodum cedit Ordinariorum locorum in munere suo rite explendo.' *Relatio super schema Decreti 'De Episcopis ac de Dioecesium regimine.'* (1963).

11. Anonymous report with SCHEMA *De pastorali Episcoporum munere in Ecclesia* (edited 1964, p. 37, n.4.h). Such a 'votum' ought to be expressed in writing since it does not follow from the diary of the Council that it should have been formulated in the oral discussions.

12. Ibid. In the Second Session (61st General Congregation, Nov.6, 1963) there had already been an intervention by Mons. Alejandro Olalia, Bishop of Lipa, made in the name of some of the Bishops of the Philippines, in which he observed that the SCHEMA should also have mentioned the rights and duties of the Papal Representatives and their relations with the Bishops in the countries where they are sent.

'Hoc magni momenti nobis videtur ut melius ac clarius definiantur eorum iura et officia et sic firmiores stabiliantur vinculo caritatis relationes inter Episcopos singulos et ipsos Legatos Romani Pontificis, in aedificationem tum cleri tum populi'.

13. *Relatio generalis de Proemio et de Capite I,* by Archbishop Petro Veuillot, edited together with *'SCHEMA decreti de pastorali Episcoporum munere in Ecclesia'. Textus recognitus et modi a commissione conciliari de Episcopis et dioecesium regimine examinati.'* Typ.Pol . Vat. (1965), p.21.

14. 'Exoptant pariter ut, ratione habita muneris pastoralis Episcoporum proprii, Legatorum Romani Pontificis officium pressius determinetur'. DECREE concerning the pastoral office of Bishops *Christus Dominus, 9 (589).*

N.B. For the conciliar and post-conciliar documents we quote the *Enchiridion Vaticanum* (EV, Edizioni Dehoniane, Bologna (1970), 9th edition, revised). In the quotations we add the marginal number of the *Enchiridion Vaticanum* (within parenthesis) to that of the paragraphs of the documents.

15. 'Optatur ut .... Legati Romani Pontificis, quantum fieri potest, ex diversis Ecclesiae regionibus magis assumantur'. *Christus Dominus,* n.10 (590).

16. 'Ob singulare quod obeunt in territorio officium, Legati Romani Pontificis non sunt de jure membra Conferentiae'. Ibid., n.38 (683).

17. Cf. nn. 21 (3152) and 28 (3162), which establish respectively the competence of the Secretariat of State and the Council for the Public Affairs of the Church. "The Apostolic Delegations", writes Laiolo, "continue, however, to depend directly also upon other Roman Congregations, that is to say, some upon the Congregation for Bishops, some upon the Congregation for Eastern Churches, and the greater part upon that for

Evangelization of Peoples." *Funzione Ecclesiale delle Rappresentanze Pontificie*, in: *La Scuola Cattolica*, 97 (1969), p. 205, note 1 bis.

18. Official text in *A.A.S.*, 61 (1969), pp. 473-484.

19. In the conciliar documents the different emphasis and the character of certain expressions which the Fathers wanted can be seen. One may compare, for example, the DE-CREE *Christus Dominus*, n.44 (699-700), where it says: "this Holy Synod directs ... orders .....". with the wording elsewhere in the same DECREE, as for instance, nn.9 (489) and 10 (592) where it is said that "The Fathers of this Holy Council express the desire .... wish .... think that it would be most useful ...".

20. EV n. 3540, *A.A.S.*, 61 (1969), p. 475.

21. C. MOELLER, *Storia della Struttura e delle idee della 'Lumen Gentium'*, in: *La Teologia dopo il Vaticano II*, Brescia (1967), p. 184.

22. *Le Statut et la Mission du Nonce*, in: *I.C.I.* (Informations Catholiques Internationales), n.336 (May 15,1968); *Supplément*, p. XIV.

23. Thus, for example, a 'Legislation' of the Church is inconceivable which is not founded on and directed by theological principles. Nor can any 'pastoral' activity be accepted, if it is not guided by theological principles.

    The Second Vatican Council, while concerning itself, to a marked degree, with the aerea of the 'pastoral', could not lessen its commitment to a task which was profoundly 'doctrinal'.

24. Cf. EV nn. 3546, 3564, 3565 (art.IV, Par. 3-4), 3574 (art.VIII, par.1), 3581 (art.X, par.2).

25. Cf. ibid., nn. 3565 (art.IV, par.4),3573 (art.VI, par. 3).

26. Cf. ibid. nn. 3571 (art.VI, par. 2b), 3573 (art.VII), 3575 (art.VIII, par. 2), 3576 (art.IX, par.1).

27. Cf. ibid. nn. 3537, 3546, 3547. This comes from the whole of the first section of the document.

28. Cf. ibid. n. 3539.

29. Cf. ibid. nn. 3539 and 3565 (art.IV, par. 4).

30. Cf. ibid. nn. 3551, 3563 (art.IV, par. 2), 3582 (art.XI, par. 1).

31. As is stated in the commentary which *IRENIKON, 42* (1969), pp. 360-361, has made on the MOTU PROPRIO in *Chronique des Eglises. Eglise Catholique.*

32. With regard to this, G. LAIOLO has noted that although the institution of Papal Representatives is only auxiliary and accidental, it is not possible to find enough space to deal with it in any notion of the Church. Consequently, there would be no place to deal with Papal Representation in an erroneous Ecclesiology which would consider the Local Church as an entity complete in itself and which contains all the theological and social realities of the Church. Nor would this be the case in an equally erroneous Ecclesiology which would consider the relationships that prosper within the Church as something purely spiritual and charismatic and not also social and juridical.

Cf. *La Funzione ecclesiale delle Rappresentante Pontifici*, in *La Scuola Cattolica*, 97 (1969), p.208 f.

33. PAUL VI, *The Opening Discourse of the Second Session of the Council* (September 29, 1963), EV n. 149*.

34. For some historical development in Ecclesiology, Cf. A. FAVALE, *Genesi della Costituzione 'Lumen Gentium'* in *La Costituzione dogmatica sulla Chiesa*, Torino-Leuman (1966), pp. 11-25.

35. PAUL VI, the Discourse quoted, EV n. 150*. For the whole section of the Discourse about the necessity of a more exact and complete definition of the Church, cf. ibid. nn. 149* - 159*.

36. Cf. M. MIDALI, *Costituzione gerarchica della Chiesa ed in modo particolare dell 'Episcopato*, in *La Costituzione dogmatica sulla Chiesa*, op. cit., p. 359.

37. THE DOGMATIC CONSTITUTION *Lumen Gentium*, Chapter I, nn. 1-8 (284-307).

38. Cf. ibid. Chapter II, nn. 9-17 (308-327).

39. Ibid. n. 9 (309).

40. Ibid. n. 8 (304).

41. Ibid. n. 1 (234) : "The Church in Christ is in the nature of a Sacrament or sign and instrument, that is, of communion with God and of unity among all men".

42. Cf. ibid. n. 9 (309-310), n. 48 (416). Cf. also the PASTORAL CONSTITUTION concerning the Church

and the Modern World *Gaudium et Spes*, n.45 (1463); the DECREE on the means of social communications *Inter Mirifica*, n. 3 (248); the DECREE dealing with the missionary activity of the Church *Ad Gentes*, n.1 (1081), n. 5 (1096); the DECREE on the Ministry and Priestly Life *Presbyterorum Ordinis*, n. 22 (1317).

43. To understand such a reassessment, it is enough to compare it with the SCHEMA of the dogmatic Constitution on the Church, prepared for examination by the Fathers of the First Vatican Council. This SCHEMA can be found in *Acta et Decreta Sacrorum Conciliorum recentium* .... ; *Coll. Lac.*, Friburgi B., Tom.VIII, a. 1890

44. *Lumen Gentium*, n. 8 (304).

45. Cf. EV n. 3548.

46. The visible character of the Church, because it is 'sui generis', cannot be judged by the stands of other visible societies. Therefore the opinion of Bellarmino may be seen to be open to criticism. This view held the Church to be "a community of men as visible and concrete as the community of the Roman people, the Kingdom of France, of the Republic of Venice." In fact, the visible character of the Church forms a part of its basic Sacramental nature; it is a "Sacramental visibility".

47. Cf. LE GUILLOU, *Le tendenze ecclesiologiche della Chiesa cattolica*, in *La fine della Chiesa come società perfetta*, Verona (1969), pp. 82-85.

48. For an attempt to present the Ecclesiology of the kind expounded by Vatican II, Cf. P. PARENTE, *Saggio di un'ecclesiologia all luce del Vaticano II, Roma (1968);*

F. HOLBOCK - TH. SARTORY, *El Misterio de la Iglesia. Fundamentos para una Ecclesiología*, 2 Vols., Barcelona (1966); PHILIPS, L'Eglise et son mystère au II Concile du Vatican, Desclée, tome I (1967), tome II (1968).

49. They can be found in: L.J. SUENENS, *Le Statut et la Mission du Nonce;* Interview in *I.C.I.*, n. 336 (May 15, 1969), *Supplément*, pp. XIII-XV; J. NEUMANN, *Neuordnung des Päpstlichen Gesandschaftswesens*, in Orientierung, 33 (1969), pp. 184-187; J. HENNESSEY *Papal Diplomacy and the Contemporary Church*, in *Thought*, 46 (1971), pp.55-71. The author maintains that Pontifical Representation is an institution in opposition to the collegiality of the Bishops. Such an idea, already presented in the interview given by Cardinal Suenens, is upheld with a polemical and journalistic slant in the article *La Nonciature après Vatican II*, in *Maintenant* (1969), n. 90. Other articles were written in a similar vein and are not worth mentioning.

The traditional difficulties about papal diplomacy can be found summarised in *Discorso di Mons. G. B. MONTINI, Sostituto della Segretaria di Stato in Occasione del 250º anniversario della Pontificia Accademia Ecclesiastica*, cf. in *Paolo VI e la Pontificia Accademia Ecclesiastica*, Poliglotta Vaticana (1965), pp. 23-57, abstract from *La Pontificia Accademia Ecclesiastica 1701-1951*, Città del Vaticano (1951), pp.XIII-XXVII, and reported in French (now out of print) by I. CARDINALE in *Le Saint Siège et la Diplomatie*, pp.183-197 - in English in *The Holy See and the International Order*, pp.295-305. The most recent objections, and those especially formulated after the Council, can be found briefly summarised by G. LAIOLO, *Funzione ecclesiale ....* , loc. cit., pp. 206 ff; and by L. DE

ECHEVERRIA, *Funciones de los Legados del Romano Pontifice,* in *Revista Española de Derecho Canónico,* XXIV (1970), pp. 586-589.

50. On the concept of 'Communio', which exists between the members of the Church and amongst the Churches, cf. G. D'ERCOLE, *Communio-Collegialità - Primato e Sollicitudo Omnium Ecclesiarum,* Roma (1964), particularly pp. 35-73 and 405-438. The author should be consulted for a more precise knowledge of his very fruitful ideas.

51. Cf. *Sollicitudo Omnium Ecclesiarum* in *Enchiridion Vaticanum (EV),* Edizioni Dehoniane, Bologna (1970), 8th edition (revised), n. .... 3552.

52. Cf. J.M. VERMULLEN, *Le MOTU PROPRIO Sollicitudo Omnium Ecclesiarum* in *Esprit et Vie* (October 9, 1969), p. 611; L. DE ECHEVERRIA, *Funciones de los Legados del Romano Pontifice (El MOTU PROPRIO Sollicitudo Omnium Ecclesiarum),* in *Revista Española de Derecho Canónico,* XXIV (1970), p. 582. Among the commentaries on the MOTU PROPRIO 'Sollicitudo Omnium Ecclesiarum', that of L. DE ECHEVERRIA (loc. cit. pp. 573-636) seems the fullest and most committed. For further consultation: M. CABREROS DE ANTA, *Las relaciones de los Legados Pontificios con los Obispos,* in *Salmanticenses,* 17 (1970), 2, pp. 417-423: F. CAVALLI, *Il MOTU PROPRIO Sollicitudo Omnium Ecclesiarum sull'ufficio dei Rappresentanti Pontifici,* in *La Civiltà Cattolica,* 120 (1969), III, pp.34-43; I. MARTIN, *Presenza della Chiesa presso gli Stati,* in *Concilium,* VI (1970), 8, pp. 113-123.

53. For example: the cc.120, par.2; 420, par. 1,6°; 1557, par.1; 1612, par.2; 2333; 2343. par.2; 2344.

127

54. *EV*. n. 3553.

55. The Council affirms that lay men "are able to be associated with the Hierarchy in the exercise of some ecclesiastical offices in order to achieve some desired spiritual goal". *Lumen Gentium*, n.33 (370). It has also determined that "henceforth ecclesiastical office ought to signify some charge given, according to an established norm, with a spiritual end in view". *Presbyterorum Ordinis*, n. 20 (1312).

After the Council, some tried to decide what office could be exercised by lay men in the context of the ecclesiastical organization; cf. for example: J. HERVADA, P. LOMBARDIA, *El Derecho del Pueblo de Dios*, I, Introduction. *La Constitucion de la Iglesia*, Pamplona (1970), pp. 358-366; O.T. REEGAN, *Les droits du laïc*, in *Concilium*, IV (1968), 8, pp. 19-29 - (the article seems to ignore the doctrine of Vatican II); P. LOMBARDIA, *Los laicos en el Derecho de la Iglesia*, in *Ius Canonicum*, VI (1966), p. 339 ff.; Item: *Los laicos*, in *Atti del Congresso Internazionale di Diritto Canonico - La chiesa dopo il Concilio*, Roma (June 14-19, 1970), 3 volumes, Milano, (1972), Vol.I (Relazioni), pp.215-243; Item: *Diritti del laico nella Chiesa*, in *Concilium*, VII (1971), 8, pp. 161-171.

The author maintains that "there is nothing in a future conception of ecclesiastical organization which would make it impossible for a lay man to exercise an office equivalent to that which is held by the Cardinal Secretary of State, or a Prefect of a Congregation of the Roman Curia, a Nuncio, or a Judge of an Ecclesiastical Court of whatever grade, given that fitness for these offices does not call for episcopal or priestly ordination but rests solely on the necessary technical competence required for these and on other suitable qualities". Ibid. p. 171.

Cardinal Suenens also asks whether it might not be better to entrust the task of diplomatic representation to lay men since this was asked for on many occasions by the Fathers of the Council. Cf. *Le Statut et las mission du Nonce*, in *Informations Catholiques Internationales, (I.C.I.)*, n. 336 (May 15, 1969), *Supplément*, p. XIV.

56. "Inhabilitas laici ad obtinendam potestatem iurisdictionis e iure positivo oritur neque etiam sic est absoluta (...). Nec desunt exempla iurisdictionis laicis concessae." A. VEERMEERSCH - I. CREUSEN, *Epitome Iuris Canonici*, Mechliniae-Romae (1963), t.I., n. 240,p.243.

57. Cf. *MOTU PROPRIO Causas Matrimoniales* (March 28, 1971), n. V, par.1, in *A.A.S.*, 63 (1971), 6, p. 443.

58. *C.I.C.*, can. 948.

59. *Lumen Gentium*, n. 10 (312).

60. "Vere, quam maxime efferendum est differentiam inter sacerdotium commune et ministeriale fundari in ordinatione sacramentali, quatenus ordinatione sacramentali confertur, cum dono Spiritus Sancti, munus et potestas sanctificandi, docendi, regendi populum Dei, scilicet facultates in ordine ad sanctificandum, docendum, regendum in Ecclesia, quae sacerdotio ministeriali institutione divina sunt specificae, ita ut qua tales in sacerdotio communi non habeantur." W. BERTRAMS, *De natura potestatis Supremi Ecclesiae Pastoris*, in *Questiones fundamentales Iuris Canonici*, Roma (1969), p. 511. Cf. also ITEM: *De quaestione circa originem potestatis*

iurisdictionis Episcoporum in Concilio Tridentino non resoluta, ibid. pp. 327-350; ITEM: *De potestatis episcopalis exercitio personali et Collegiali*, ibid. pp. 388-408 (especially pp. 389-396); W. ONCLIN, *Le pouvoir de l'Evêque et le principe de la collégialité*, a paper given to the International Congress of Canon Law (Rome, January 14-19, 1970), cf. in *Atti del Congresso ....*, op. cit., vol.I, pp. 135-161.

61. The opinion that a Bishop-elect does not possess of his own the potestas of his office until he is ordained a Bishop, and that the Bishop-elect of Rome does not have full primatial power if he is not ordained Bishop, is shared by many, particularly after the Second Vatican Council. The Council expressed itself in quite a solemn way about the sacramentality of power in the Church (whether one speaks of the unicity of power and plurality of functions, or whether one prefers to express it in terms of potestates).

On this subject cf. PHILIPS, *L'Eglise et son mystère au IIe Concile du Vatican*, t. I, (1967), p. 256; U. BETTI, *La dottrina sull'episcopato nel capitolo III della Costituzione dommatica 'Lumen Gentium'*, Roma (1968), p. 356 f. This opinion is sustained in an authoritative manner by BERTRAMS, *De natura potestatis Supremi Ecclesiae Pastoris*, loc. cit., in which he affirms that "non sufficit determinatio iuridica potestatis ad constituendam potestatem ante consecrationem". Ibid. p. 517, note 14 (where he cites PHILIPS and BETTI). He concludes "Supremus Ecclesiae Pastor non est plene creatus, potestas primatialis in subiecto canonice designato ad officium S. Petri, non est ex integro constituta, quamdiu in ipso consecratio episcopalis desideratur". ibid. p. 520.

With regard to this, the APOSTOLIC CONSTITUT-

ION *Romano Pontifici Eligendo* (October 1, 1975), must be cited. In n. 88 it states: "Post acceptationem, electus qui episcopali ordinatione iam pollet, est illico Romanae Ecclesiae Episcopus simulque verus Papa, et Caput Collegii Episcopalis; idemque actu plenam et supremam potestatem in universam Ecclesiam acquirit atque exercere potest. Quodsi electus charactere episcopali careat, statim ordinetur Episcopus,". *A.A.S.*, LXVIII (1975), p. 664. Arguing 'e contrario', it could be inferred that a Pope-elect, who is not already ordained Bishop, is not immediately "Romanae Ecclesiae Episcopus, verus Papa, Caput Collegii Episcopalis", and does not at once possess "plenam et supremam potestatem in universam Ecclesiam,". But it is quite possible that what this document wishes to do is to make a positive affirmation, without denying the contrary.

The fact that the person who has been elected Pope might be everything that is described in the Constitution, when such conditions are present, does not exclude the possibility that he may have the same "supremam auctoritatem" when some of these conditions are lacking. It would seem justifiable to maintain that the document has no intention of explicitly excluding the contrary of its affirmative statements. In fact, it did not intend putting an end to the different theological opinions which exist with regard to this question.

62. *Christus Dominus,* n. 11 (593). Cf. *Lumen Gentium,* n. 20 (333), nn. 28-29 (354-260).

63. The possibility that eventually some of the priests who work in the Roman Congregations or in the Diocesan Curias, might be replaced by lay persons, should not be dismissed. This is because in some instances there is

nothing in their work which is a genuine sharing in the "munus et potestas" of the Bishop of the Apostolic See or of the Pastors of particular Churches.

64. *Lumen Gentium,* n.31 (363).

65. Ibid., n. 10 (312).

66. Cf. ibid., n. 32 (366).

67. Cf. ibid., n. 33 (370).

68. About this question, see: G. LAIOLO, *Funzione ecclesiale delle Rappresentanze Pontificie,* art. cit., p. 230 ff.

69. P. CIPROTTI *(Funzione e valore della S. Sede,* in: *Concilium,* VI (1970), 8, p. 88) is not convincing when he maintains that the Holy See acts both as an organ of the Catholic Church and as an instrument of the Vatican City State, when it sends or receives diplomatic representatives, and he adds that "it is certainly true that by far the most important function of these diplomatic representatives is that which is concerned with ecclesiastical matters ".

For I. CARDINALE, in: *Le Saint-Siège et la diplomatie,* op. cit., p. 85, the Pope has the right to legislate by reason of a two-fold juridical capacity, spiritual and temporal, as Head of the Church and Sovereign of the Vatican City State as well. According to the author, therefore, we ought to expect a two-tiered system of representation: spiritual and temporal. Instead, the same diplomatic envoy exercises the normal functions of representing the two sovereignties.

P. BLET, *Le antiche Nunziature,* in: "L'Osservatore

Romano" (July 2, 1969), does not hesitate to state that "there is no doubt that nuncios also represent the Pope as a temporal sovereign".

I. MARTIN, *Presenza della Chiesa presso gli Stati,* in *Concilium,* VI (1970) 8, p. 115, holds that before 1870 Legates of the Supreme Pontiff were undoubtedly sent by the Supreme Authority of the Church and also were Envoys of the Sovereign of State (the Pontifical State, which was one amongst the other States); during the period of the Roman Question (1870-1929) they retained only the first characteristic. Then, after the creation of the Vatican City State by the Lateran Treaty, some uncertainty about the position developed.

We do not even wish to consider the position of those who maintain that Nuncios should be considered merely as Ambassadors of the Vatican. Rather, we think that the opinion of G. LAIOLO (art. cit., p.221), is more in keeping with the actual facts. He maintains that the terminus a quo of the diplomatic representation, established by the despatch of a Nuncio to a Government, is the Supreme Pontiff, in so far as he is the supreme visible Authority of the Catholic Church. Nunciatures are not dependent upon the Roman Pontiff in his capacity as Sovereign of the Vatican City State; (he adds: "this does not lessen the power of the Holy See to deal with the few affairs connected with the Vatican City State through the Nunciatures as well"). Besides the autonomy of the Vatican City as a State, as appears without any ambiguity from its very creation, depends upon the spiritual sovereignty of the Holy See, and is totally at its service. According to the author, Nuncios therefore, always represent, immediately, the Holy See, but mediately and ultimately, the Church.

133

After the MOTU PROPRIO *Sollicitudo Omnium Ecclesiarum* this view seems unquestionable, since in the document the Pope expressly states that the sending of his own Legates to the supreme Authorities of Nations is "by native right, inherent in our very spiritual mission and favoured by the centuries-old development of historical events." It is precisely in so far as he is Supreme Pastor of the Church that the Pope has a spiritual mission, and as such that he sends his Representatives to the States.

His temporal sovereignty of the Vatican City State has no other justification for its existence than that of making it possible for him to exercise more freely his spiritual mission. And since it has no other reason for existing except as an instrument, as an *esse ad* (being for), the more logical position would appear to be that sustained by G. IANNACCONE, *La Personalità Giuridica Internazionale della Chiesa,* in: *Il Diritto Ecclesiastico,* 41 (1930), pp. 435-443. He maintains that the Vatican City State does not possess a proper personality of its own in the International Community, but is rather an attribute or necessary means, created by reason of a bilateral Agreement in favour of an already-existent subject in international law, that is to say, the Catholic Church.

If in a new arrangement of the International Community, the independence of the Apostolic See could be as equally well guaranteed as it is by the Vatican City State, then this "miniscule, almost symbolic temporal sovereignty" of the Holy See could even disappear. Similar opinions are held by J. CALVO OTERO in: *Relazioni moderne fra Chiesa e Stato......* art. cit., in: *Concilium,* VI (1970) 8, p. 146. For a rather more recent opinion about the international personality of the Vatican City, see: J. PUENTE EGIDO, *Personalidad internacional de la Ciudad del Vaticano*, Madrid 1965.

70. Cf. WERNZ, *Ius Decretalium*, Prati 1915, t. II, n. 688, pp. 468-471.

71. Ibid., p. 469.

72. Cf. R.A. GRAHAM, *Vatican Diplomacy*, Princeton 1959, p. 123.

73. Graham states: "from the beginning the Nuncios were almost without exception ecclesiastics and not laymen... In the whole history of papal diplomacy the number of laymen employed on diplomatic missions is infinitesimal." (Op. cit., p. 123). Moreover, the author finds it natural that the Representatives of the Pope should be Ecclesiastics, and this for two reasons:

    1) Because the person whom they are representing is first and foremost a Religious Authority: "The Nuncios' quality should correspond to that of their Chief".

    2) Because the Nuncio, from the very beginning, was entrusted with the exercise of ecclesiastical functions and not merely with dealing with political questions. In many cases, the Nuncio enjoyed canonical jurisdiction delegated by the Pope. It was, therefore, suitable that the Envoy should be a Cleric. Cf. ibid. p. 124.

135

74. *La presenza della Santa Sede negli organismi internazionali*, in: *Concilium*, VI (1970) 8, p. 109.

75. Ibid., p. 112.

76. Cf. M. FLICK, *La Pontificia Accademia Ecclesiastica*, art. cit., p. 531 f.

77. H. BIAUDET, *Les Nonciatures apostoliques permanentes jusq'en 1648*, Helsinki 1910, p. 41.

78. Cf. Ibid., pp. 41-47.

79. Cf. L. DE ECHEVERRIA, art. cit., p. 593.

80. Cf. *Lumen Gentium*, n.29 (336).

81. Cf. G. LAIOLO, *Funzione ecclesiale ...* art. cit., p. 231. As I. GORDON writes: "Episcopatus in Curia Romana non solum est honor, verum etiam ut munus confertur, siquidem Praelati Superiores Curiae Romanae, qui charactere episcopali gaudent, aptiores sunt ex natura Episcopatus ad collaborandum cum Romano Pontifice in cura pastorali Ecclesiae universae; eoque magis quia, iuxta aliquorum Patrum desiderium Curiae Romanae actio magis pastoralis evadere deberet." *De Curia Romana renovata*, in: *Periodica*, 58 (1969), p.100.

82. *Christus Dominus*, n. 25 (636). It does not seem necessary to restrict the Episcopal Ordination of those who are not actually Pastors of Churches in order to be able to speak of an effective renewal of Local Churches. This is the position of H. M. LEGRAND, *Implicazione teologica della rivalorizzazione delle Chiese locali* in: *Concilium*,

VIII (1927) 1, 82. Among the examples of those who are not to be given Episcopal Ordination the author places Cardinals, Nuncios, and members of the Curia.

83. We do not wish to deal with the question of whether or not Pontifical Legations enjoy juridical personality. Some treatment of this is given in: J. SABATIER, *Revision de estructuras ecclesiasticas: personas morales,* in: *Ius Canonicum,* X (1970), p. 122 f.

84. The two terms, Legate and Representative, are used here without distinction. The Latin text always has Legatus, which is consistently translated in Italian as Rappresentante. The first term stresses the aspect of Mission (of being sent), while the second highlights the content and aims of the Mission ... that is ad repraesentandum.

85. In the light of this, it is more easily understandable why a Legation, both to the Local Churches and to the States is given to one and the same person; at the same time the preoccupation of those who consider the union of these two functions to be such that the mission to the States contaminates that to the Churches is overcome. So, for example, Cardinal Suenens: "L'alliance de ces deux fonctions fait problème." This is even more true, as far as he is concerned, as he makes the statement that the diplomatic function of the Nuncio makes him an Ambassador of the Vatican. Cf. *Le Statut et la mission du Nonce,* Interview in: *I.C.I., Supplément,* n. 336 (May 15, 1969), p. xiv.

From the very beginnings of permanent Nunciatures and throughout their history, as long as the Nuncios were also entrusted - until the fall of the Papal States - with political functions, the custom never existed of confiding the two functions to two different persons.

86. Because such a subdistinction is not of substantial importance but belonging to one or other category can assume a particular significance according to circumstances, we shall limit ourselves to examining that particular significance, while mentioning other studies which develop this point. So, for example, see: I. CARDINALE, *Le Saint-Siège et la Diplomatie*, op. cit., pp. 92-105; (in: *The Holy See and the International Order*, pp. 140-152); L. DE ECHEVERRIA, *Funciones de los Legados del Romano Pontifice*, art. cit., in: *Revista Española de Derecho Canónico*, XXIV (1970), pp. 592-605.

87. For an evaluation of the Convention see A. MARESCA, *La convenzione di Vienna sulle relazioni diplomatiche*, in: *La Comunità internazionale*, XVI (1961) 2, pp.247-273. Item: *Introduzione alla "Convenzione di Vienne sulle relazioni diplomatiche"*, a publication of the Italian Society for International Organization, Document-XIII, Padova, 1961, pp. IX-XV; SANZ VILLALBA, *La Conferencia de Viena sobre relaciones diplomaticas*, in: *Revista Española de Derecho Canónico*, 16 (1961), pp. 119-126; COLLIARD, *La Convention de Vienne sur les relations diplomatiques*, in: *Annuaire Francais de droit international*, 1961.

88. Art. 14, par.1: "Les Chefs de mission sont repartis en trois classes, à savoir: a) celle des Ambassadeurs ou Nonces accrédités auprès des Chefs d'Etat et des autres Chefs de mission ayant un rang equivalent; b) celle des Envoyés, Ministres ou Internonces accrédités auprès des Chefs d'Etat; c) celle des Chargés d'affaires accrédités auprès des Ministères des Affaires Etrangères."

89. Cf. A. MARESCA, *La Convenzione di Vienna*, loc. cit., p. 257, n. 13, 6.

90. Cf. "L'Osservatore Romano" of October 28, 1965.

91. Art. 16, par.1: "Les Chefs de mission prennent rang dans chaque classe suivant la date et l'heure à laquelle ils ont assumé leurs fonctions conformement à l'article 13.

Par.2: ....

Par. 3: Le présent article n'affecte pas les usages qui sont ou seraient acceptés par l'Etat accréditaire en ce qui concerne la preséance du Représentant du Saint-Siége."

A. MARESCA writes: "The approval of the scheme concerning the precedence of the Holy See's Representative and the amendment proposed by the pontifical delegation - the approval came, after a long series of heated declarations of support, by a unanimous vote of the delegates, with the sole declared abstention from the Communist States - constituted one of the highest spiritual moments in the Conference's history." *La Convenzione di Vienna*, loc. cit., p. 257.

92. For a further account of the principles involved, see: I. CARDINALE, op., cit. pp. 109-118. Actually, the matter is theoretical since while the possibility of nominating Internuncios remains, in fact, such an office has disappeared following the advent of Pronuncios who, in recent years, have become quite numerous. On the other hand, there was a proposal put forward by some delegations to suppress the categories of Envoys, Ministers and Internuncios, given the progressive disappearance of legations. Cf. MARESCA. Loc. cit., p. 256, n. 13, 1.

Finally, it ought to be said that at the time of the Vienna Convention on Diplomatic

Relations it was not possible to speak about the custom of giving Internuncios rights of precedence since the Holy See nominated Internuncios precisely in those countries with whom it was possible to establish diplomatic relations, but who did not wish to guarantee a privileged position to the Holy See's Representative.

93. Cf. ERNESTO GALLINA, *I Pro-Nunzi-Apostolici*, in: *L'Osservatore Romano*, October 28, 1965, p.2; K. WALF, *Der Apostolische Pronuntius. Neue Sinngebung für einen alten Terminus Technicus*, in: *Archives für Katholisches Kirchenrecht*, 134 (1965), pp. 376-381.

94. Cf. L. DE ECHEVERRIA, *Las funciones* ... loc. cit., p. 594.

95. A propos the right of precedence, ERNESTO GALLINA writes: "The justification for this rests, and particularly so, upon the fact that amongst the bodies which make up the international community, the Holy See, and it alone, is distinguished by its special nature and by very particular characteristics which determine its goals and activity. These three - nature, goals and activity - refer directly to whatever is considered most noble by all men; the totality of spiritual and moral values." *I Pro-Nunzi Apostolici*, loc. cit.

96. *The Church and the International Community*, in: *Atti del Congresso*, op. cit., vol. I, p. 448.

97. *Annuario Pontificio 1967*, p. 1001.

98. *L'Osservatore Romano*, August 15, 1970.

99. I. CARDINALE, op. cit., p. 99; DE ECHEVERRIA loc. cit., p. 598.

100. For a further treatment, cf. I. CARDINALE, Ibid., p. 98f; L. DE ECHEVERRIA, Ibid., p. 599.

101. Cf. art. II, par.3; Ev, n. 3558.

102. For the concepts of an International Conference and Congress, and their minor differences and structure, cf. E. SATOW, *A Guide to Diplomatic Practice*, New York, 1962 (4th ed. revised), pp. 303-314. For the origin and development of the *Presence of the Holy See in International Bodies*, see the article cited of H. DE RIEDMATTEN in: *Concilium*, IV (1920),pp. 91-112.

103. G. OLIVERO, *La Chiesa e la Comunità internazionale*, loc. cit., p. 451. J. M. CASTAÑO has devoted a study to this problem, *Puede la Iglesia formar parte de la O.N.U.?*, in: *Atti del Congresso*, op. cit., vol. II *(Communicationes)*, pp. 295-323, especially pp. 320-323. Bearing in mind that both the specific nature of the Church and the 'Charter of San Francisco' he concludes: "Ahora bien, la Iglesia, por exigencias de su naturaleza, no es un Estado; pertenece a un orden diverso del orden temporal en el que se mueven todos los entes internacionales, includia la O.N.U., y por consiguiente, no tiene derecho a ser miembro de derecho de la Organizacion de las Naciones Unidas ". Earlier he had stated and demonstrated that it is not sufficient to be an "international person" in order to possess the prerogative of being a member by right of O.N.U., but it must also possess the characteristics required by the specific legislation of the organization.

104. Art. 19 of Vienna Convention on Diplomatic Relations establishes the manner of procedure with the Foreign Ministry when a Charge d'Affaires

'ad interim' assumes his provisional functions.

105. "Romano Pontifici ius nativum et independens competit Legatos suos libere nominandi, mittendi, transferendi et revocandi, servatis normis iuris internationalis, quod attinet ad missionem et revocationem Legatorum apud Res Publicas constitutorum." Not only the second part of this paragraph but also the terminology which is used in the first section shows a greater influence of International Law than that of Canon Law.

106. Art. 2 of the Vienna Convention on Diplomatic Relations says: "L'etablissement de relations diplomatiques entre Etats et l'envoi de missions diplomatiques permanentes se font pars consentment mutuel." It is possible to speak of bilateral agreement from which each party could withdraw without violating the rights of the other.

107. It should be stressed as a matter of considerable importance that in all these articles the term Pontifical Representative is always used without specifying whether or not it has a diplomatic character. It must be concluded, then, that the functions laid down in the MOTU PROPRIO apply to a l l Representatives, bearing in mind, however, that the duties which are connected with relations with the Political Community will develop with a particular expression, force and juridical importance when they are exercised by a Legate who has diplomatic capacity.

108. Referring particularly to this paragraph, the commentators of the MOTU PROPRIO stress that the function of the Pontifical Representative with regard to Local Churches, is of prime importance, whereas in the past the stress was rather on his diplomatic role. One notes,

for example, DE ECHEVERRIA, *Las funciones ...,* loc. cit., p. 613. He states, among other things, that the MOTU PROPRIO, in describing "las actividades de las representaciones pontificias, insiste, en el aspecto pastoral, dejando en un segundo plano, relegado al art. 10, el aspecto diplomatico", ibid., p. 613; M. CABREROS DE ANTA, *Las relaciones de los Legados Pontificios con los Obispos,* in: *Salmanticenses,* 17 (1970) 2, p. 417 ff., where he speaks of the "supremacy of the Pastoral over the Diplomatic Function".

There is, surely, no doubt that according to the *Sollicitudo Omnium Ecclesiarum,* the principal task, the preeminent function of any Pontifical Representative - even one who has a diplomatic capacity - , is directed to the Local Churches: the Pontifical Legate is primarily seen as such within the Church (Legation *ad intra*); however, that does not imply any reduction in his function with regard to the Political Community, a function which, among other things, is to a great extent of concern to all Representatives, as was noted above (n.107), and this applies also to those not appointed with diplomatic capacity.

We have already clearly expressed our opinion about the activities of the Pontifical Representatives towards the Political Community and the special significance they acquire when they are able to act on the diplomatic level. It is important to reaffirm that we consider the relations with the Political Community on the part of the Legate of the Holy See to be of a religious and ecclesial nature. Those contacts can also be described as a pastoral function, in the sense that they belong to the activities of the Church ad extra. It cannot be called pastoral, if with the term you intend something which effectively has to do with the *auctoritas gubernandi vel regendi,* which exists within the Church. 'Pastoral' in this sense can be considered, at least not strictly speaking, the function with regard to the Local Churches; (it should not be forgotten that the purpose of the legislation of the MOTU PROPRIO is "to place in the proper light, within the context of the Church's organs of government, the functions of Pontifical Representatives." *EV,* n. 3552).

For that reason, even though we fully agree with those writers who consider that functions concerned with Local Churches are of primary importance, we cannot quite see why those should be the only ones to be considered 'pastoral', unless we accept that a 'pastoral' activity can exist only within the Church. We would definitely call the mission to the Local Churches a religious-ecclesial-pastoral function *ad intra,* the mission to the Political Community a religious-ecclesial-pastoral function *ad extra* with or without diplomatic capacity.

109. "Pontificius Legatus, pro suo ordinario munere, debet Apostolicam Sedem certo tempore, ex veritate et aequitate certiorem facere de condicionibus in quibus versantur Ecclesiae ad quas missus est, deque omnibus illis quae ipsam vitam Ecclesiae et bonum animarum contingunt". *EV.* n.3568.

110. It must be admitted that the rulings of the MOTU PROPRIO sometimes lack force and juridical coherence. Therefore, in the revised Canon Law they should not appear as at present stated, but possibly in a form which would be more precise juridically.

111. We think that the word 'vigilantia' has been avoided so

far, perhaps in order to eliminate the idea of sole control, which is too restrictive, and to attach instead to the informative functions its complete depth of meaning: and this implies that the problem and the life of the Local Churches should be lived, and not merely observed from without, in a spirit of detachment and with the approach of an outsider.

The concept of 'vigilantia' in its full and true sense, cannot exclude citizenship within the Church; it is one of the functions of the Bishop - (let us not forget the original meaning of the word: 'Inspector') - with regard to his Church, and of the Bishop of the Apostolic See with regard to all the Churches. For the rest the function of 'vigilantia' was entrusted to Vicars and Legates from the earliest days, and it cannot but remain.

112. "Legatus Pontificius, hinc quidem Apostolicae Sedi nuntiat Episcoporum, Cleri, Religiosorum Laicorumque fidelium sui territorii consilia et vota; inde verum actorum, documentorum, notitiarum mandatorumque, quae ab Apostolica Sede procedunt interpres fit apud illos ad quos eadem spectant." *EV.* n. 3568.

113. "Quare singula Dicasteria atque Officia Curiae Romanae Pontificio Legato captas deliberationes significare non omittent ac plerumque ipsius opera utentur, ut deliberationes ad eos, quorum interest, perveniant; itidem etiam Legatum Pontificum consultent circa ea negotia ac decreta, quae ad territorium attinent, in quo ipse degit." *EV.* n. 3569.

114. Regarding the functions of the Pontifical Representative in the matter of Episcopal nominations, there is also a statement of one of the fourteen final resolutions of the

European Meeting of Delegates of the National Councils of Priests (Geneva, April 20 - 23, 1971). We reproduce it here (translated into English), according to the text of the *La Civilta Cattolicà*, 1971, p. 380 f., footnote 18. Resolution n. 12: "In the choice of Bishops the Pope and the Roman Authorities should make direct contact with the Dioceses concerned. The Apostolic Nuncio, being a diplomat accredited to the Government, is not competent in these matters and should be considered as having no responsibility in local affairs,"; 43 yes; 9 iuxta modum; 8 against; 2 null.

The reason given to exclude the Nuncios from competence in the nomination of Bishops and every responsibility in the life of Local Churches, shows clearly the desire to restrict the mission of the Papal Representative to a *purely diplomatic role,* withholding from him any function connected with the Churches. This means a repetition of attempts already carried out in the past, (nothing is new in the history of the Church!), and shows a stubborn opposition to the tasks which, under the legislation in force, are by the Apostolic See committed to its Representatives, with or without diplomatic capacity.

115. "Firmo manente iure Romani Pontificis nominandi et instituendi Episcopos, et salva disciplina Ecclesiarum Orientalium, Conferentiae Episcopales, iuxta normas ab Apostolica Sede statutas vel statuendas, de viris ecclesiasticis ad Episcoptatus Officium in Proprio territorio promovendis prudenti consilio sub secreto quotamnis agant et candidatorum nomina Apostolicae Sedi proponant." *Ecclesiae Sanctae,* n. 10 (2222).

This article was applied by means of a document of the Council for the Public Affairs of the Church, bearing the date of March 25, 1972. Cf. in: *A.A.S.*, LXIV (1972) pp. 386-391: "De promovendis ad Episcopatum in Ecclesia Latina. Normae de promovendis ad Episcopale ministerium in Ecclesia latina." So far as the role of the Pontifical Representative is concerned, reference should be made to Articles XII (informative canonical processes on the candidates) and XIII (report on the "statu et necessitatibus" of the Diocese "providenda"), not to mention Article VI, which in paragraph 2 lists the qualities required of candidates for the Episcopate.

116. Cf. *Christus Dominus*, n. 20 (622). Among the most solemn declarations of the "Sacrosancta Oecumenica Synodus", there is specifically that one which states: "The competent Ecclesiastical Authority has the proper, special and, as of right, exclusive power to appoint and install Bishops".

117. Such a right is laid down in the MOTU PROPRIO *Cleri Sanctitati* (June 11, 1957), especially cc. 251-255 .

118. "Firmis manentibus partibus Conferentiarum Episcopalium quoad expromenda vota et consilia de erectione, dismembratione et suppressione dioecesium vel provinciarum ecclesiasticarum, et salva ecclesiarum Orientalium disciplina, Legatus Pontificius harum quaestionum studium, ubi opus, ipse promoveat et quid Conferentia Episcopalis de hac re proponat, una cum proprio voto, competenti Apostolicae Sedis Dicasterio significet." *EV.* n. 3573.

119. C. 215, paragraph 1, of *C.I.C.* is still in force: "Unius supremae ecclesiasticae potestatis est provincias ecclesiasticas, dioeceses, abbatias vel praelaturas nullius, vicariatus apostolicos, praefecturas apostolicas erigere, aliter cirumscribere, dividere, unire, supprimere"; as

well as c. 159 of MOTU PROPRIO *Cleri Sanctitati:* "Erectio seu restitutio, immutatio et suppressio patriarchatuum, archiepiscopatuum, provinciarum,eparchiarum, exarchiarum cum territorio proprio aut apostolicarum competit Romano Pontifici vel Oecumenicae Synodo, salvo praescripto c. 248; 327, par.1; 328".

120. Cf. nn. 22-24 (624-634) and nn. 39-41 (690-694).

121. Cf. art. 12 (2225-2226) and art. 42 (2306).

122. Cf. MOTU PROPRIO *Cleri Sanctitati,* cc. 159; 248; 327 and 1: 328.

123. "Quod attinet ad rationes habendas cum Episcopis, quibus ex divino mandato animorum cura in singulis dioecesibus commissa est, Legatus Pontificius, integrum relinquens Episcopis eorum iurisdictionis exercitium, iis opem ferre, consilia dare, prompte generoseque suam operam praestare debet, fraterno consociatae operae spiritu permotus". EV, n. 3574.

124. As for example the functions described in the MOTU PROPRIO *Pastorale Munus* (November 30, 1963). On this point J.H. Vermullen states: "On pourrait, peut-être souhaiter que les nonces (not only Nuncios but all Papal Representatives) obtiennent, par la suite, des facultés spéciales réalisant une plus réelle décentralisation des dicastères romains, notamment dans le déroulement des causes d'annulations de mariages (dispenses pour non-consommation, obtention du privilège pétrinien en cas de mariages dispars ...). Les justiciables y auraient grand intérêt." *Esprit et Vie,* October 9, 1969, 612.

125. On these principles, the MOTU PROPRIO has already

spoken in the explanatory - doctrinal section, at the point where it quotes the text of St. Gregory the Great: "Si sua unicuique episcopo iurisdictio non servetur, quid aliud agitur nisi ut per nos, per quos ecclesiasticus custodiri debuit ordo confundatur ?" *EV*, n. 3546.

126. *Las relaciones de los Legados Pontificios con los Obispos*. in: *Salmanticenses*, 17 (1970) 2, pp. 419-423.

127. Ibid., p. 421.

128. It is useful in this connection to refer to the words directed by Paul VI to the Pontifical Representatives in the various Nations of Asia. Having said that in the past the function of the Nuncio towards the Churches "was above all hierarchical and administrative, and he remained, to a certain extent, a body outside the Local Church", the Pope added: "Today, instead, the Nuncio should bring to his function a more marked pastoral tendency, because, he also is at the service of the Kingdom of God which flourishes in the country concerned". He goes on to say that the Pontifical Representative should represent, in dealing with the local Hierarchies, the "living sign" of the communion and solidarity which exists amongst the Bishops and with the Bishop of Rome, on the basis of collegiality, which is "charity and, in some measure, co-responsibility"; and, moreover, he should share, as far as possible, the pastoral concern of the Bishops.

The Pontifical Representatives are "the witnesses of the catholicity and universality of the Christian Message", and represent "the need for unity in the diversity of expression of the same faith", forming, "so to speak, the *trait d'union* between the Local Churches throughout the whole world." He concludes by asserting: "This cannot be envisaged without a more fraternal contact with the life of the Local Churches", which it is up to the Representative to carry out in each case in accordance with concrete methods, "in the spirit of an authentic service and in the knowledge that he - the Pontifical Representative - is before all else a bond of charity."

129. Cf. *Christus Dominus*, nn. 37-38 (681-689). It may be pointed out, however, that neither the theological nor the juridical nature of such an institution had yet been fully determined. There have been numerous studies on this in the post-Council period. The danger of over-evaluation of such an institution should not be overlooked, as this would risk harming the initiative and autonomy of every Bishop.

DE LUBAC states: "The primary purpose of Episcopal Conferences is on the practical level and their effectiveness depends on the limitation of this purpose. Their work does not normally constitute in itself an exercise of collegiality. ' Lumen Gentium ' recognizes no doctrinal intermediary between the Local and the Universal Church. It would amount to corruption of an excellent institution, and one which is supremely opportune, but not totally essential, if it were to be confused to a greater or lesser extent with the institution of the Episcopal College". *Local Churches and the Universal Church*, in *L'Osservatore Romano*, November 2-3, 1971, p.3.

130. Cf. article 41, EV, nn. (2296-2305).

131. *Christus Dominus*, n. 38 (683).

132. *Archetypon Statuti Conferentiae Episcoporum*, cf. in *Periodica*, 57 (1968), pp. 227-280.

133. Information on this can be found in : L. DE ECHEVER-RIA, *Funciones de los Legados del Romano Pontefice*, loc. cit., p. 625.

134. In certain specific cases the MOTU PROPRIO requires the Representative to take note of the Episcopal Conference; for example, in matters relating to candidates for the Episcopate (Article VI, 2, b), Ecclesiastical Areas (Article VII), Agreements, Negotiations, Concordats, Conventions, Modus vivendi (Article X, 2), etc.

135. C. 488, 3°, of *C.I.C.* defines the 'religio iuris pontificii' as 'religio quae vel approbationem vel saltem laudis decretum ab Apostolica Sede est consecuta'.

136. The Decree *Perfectae Caritatis* has encouraged union between Religious Institutes, and this union can assume the various forms of 'federation', 'union', 'association'. Cf. n. 22 (764).

137. Major Superiors are, according to c. 488, 8°, of *C.I.C.*: "Abbas Primas, Abbas Superior Congregationis monasticae, Abbas monasterii sui iuris, licet ad monasticam Congregationem pertinentis, supremus religionis Moderator, Superior provincialis, eorundem Vicarii aliique ad instar provincialium, potestatem habentes".

138. The Council has declared that encouragement should be given to the Conferences or Councils of Major Superiors, as set up by the Holy See. Such Conferences will have the function of aiding individual Institutes to pursue their aim more effectively, to promote better collaboration between the Institutes for the good of the Church,

to distribute more practically the 'workers' for the Gospel, to deal with the questions which the Religious have in common and also to set up a suitable system of coordination and collaboration with the Episcopal Conferences in all that concerns the exercise of the Apostolate. Cf. *Perfectae Caritatis*, 23 (765).

In the Decree *Ad Gentes*, having previously stated that between Institutes which carry out missionary activities in the same territory there should exist a coordination of work, the great value of Conferences of Religious and Unions of Sisters to which all Institutes of the same Nation or Region should belong, is affirmed in this connection. Such Conferences should maintain close contact with the Episcopal Conferences. Cf. also *Christus Dominus*, n. 35, 5° (677); the rules of enforcement are contained in the MOTU PROPRIO *Ecclesiae Sanctae*, articles 42-43, (2362-2364), article 21 (2404). The Apostolic Constitution *Regimini Ecclesiae Universae*, n.73, paragraph 5 (3247) lays down that it is the responsibility of the Sacred Congregation for the Religious and Secular Institutes " to set up Councils or Conferences of Major Superiors, whose activities it will ensure are put to the best use".

139. *Christus Dominus*, n. 35, 5° (676).

140. As, for example, L. DE ECHEVERRIA, *'Funciones ... ';* loc. cit., p. 627.

141. L.J. SUENENS, *Le Statut et la Mission du Nonce,* loc. cit., p. XIV.

142. It has already been said that the legislation of the MOTU PROPRIO speaks indistinctly of *munera* of the Pontifical Representative, without specifying whether it is deal-

ing with those with diplomatic capacity or otherwise, except, perhaps in Article X. The functions, therefore, laid down by the MOTU PROPRIO apply to all Papal Legates, so that it would not have been necessary to specify it even in this case. Here, however, the ruling is explicit.

143. *Sollicitudo Omnium Ecclesiarum,* (Doctrinal Section), *EV,* n. 3549.

144. The expression "to whom he is accredited" ("apud quam 'nationem' legationem suam exercet") leads one to think that it refers to Representatives with diplomatic capacity. The ruling could certainly have been more explicit (if it was meant to apply only to diplomatic Representatives, it might have mentioned Nuncios, Pro-Nuncios and Inter-Nuncios), especially if one considers that it says in Article IV that even non-diplomatic Representatives should make a point of promoting friendly and useful relations with the Civil Authorities.

Besides, the functions laid down by Article X can (and sometimes must) be carried out also by the Legate who is not officially accredited to the State, always provided:
1) that any action of his is on a different level and differs juridically from that of the diplomatic Representative;

2) that the function "to concern himself particularly with the stipulation of 'modus vivendi', of agreements and concordats, as well as of conventions referring to questions within the sphere of public law" can be regarded as 'ordinaria' in the case of a diplomatic Representative; it should,

153

however be determined in each individual case when a non-diplomatic Representative is involved. This, we think, can be deduced from the legislation in force, provided that Article X of the MOTU PROPRIO deals only with diplomatic Representatives; there are good reasons to maintain that this is so.

145. Article II, paragraph 3 states that "the norms contained in this document do not concern the Delegates and Observers of the Holy See . . ., unless expressly mentioned". *EV*, 3558.

146. C. 1188, paragraph 1 of *C.I.C.* defines the concept of 'Oratory': "Est locus divino cultui destinatus, non tamen eo potissimum fine ut universo fidelium populo usui sit ad religionem publice colendam".

147. C. 268, paragraph 3 of *C.I.C.* states instead: "Si charactere episcopali sint aucti ...."; whereas c. 215 of the MOTU PROPRIO *Cleri Sanctitati* says: "Etsi charactere episcopali carent ....". Here it was no longer necessary to be specific; in fact the Pontifical Representative is normally endowed with episcopal dignity.

148. Therefore he reserves the right of precedence over Patriarchs of the Western Churches and also over Primates.

149. As for the rest, diplomatic immunities, prerogatives and privileges, as established by International Law, aim essentially at fostering a proper accomplishment of the diplomatic mission.

150. After the Second Vatican Council, for example, the

Sacred Congregation for the Evangelization of Peoples issued a *List of Faculties,* which are customarily granted to Nuncios, Pro-Nuncios and Apostolic Delegates: *Index Facultatum Nuntiis, Pro-Nuntiis at Delegatis Apostolics in Territoriis Missionum tributarum* (1971).

The List of Faculties contains twenty three items. Moreover, in the *Animadversiones* it is stated that "pariter conceduntur facultates omnes in Litteris Apostolicis Motu Proprio datis Pastorale Munus contentae necnon Facultates Decennales Sacrae Congregationis pro Gentium Evangelizatione seu de Propaganda Fide." (Article 1). In the other articles of the *Animadversiones* the conditions and details regarding the exercise of these Faculties are laid down.

Similar Faculties are also granted by the Sacred Congregation for Bishops, *Index Facultatum Nuntiis, Inter-Nuntiis et Delegatis Apostolicis Tributarum* (1968), and by the Sacred Congregation for Eastern Churches, *Facultates Legatis Romani Pontificis Concessae* (1975), for the territories of their respective jurisdiction.

Apostolic Letter
of
Paul VI
Supreme Pontiff
on The Duties of Pontifical Representatives
'Sollicitudo Omnium Ecclesiarum'

The care of all the Churches, to which We have been called by the hidden design of God and for which We must one day give an account, requires that, as Vicar of Christ, We should be adequately present in all parts of the world and be informed about the state and condition of each Church.

For the Bishop of Rome, by reason of his office, 'has full, supreme and universal power, which he can always freely exercise' (1), since it is both ordinary and immediate (2). Moreover, 'as the successor of Peter, he is the perpetual and visible source and foundation of the unity both of the bishops and of the whole company of the faithful' (3). Amongst these he has, therefore, the principal role in ensuring 'that the Episcopate should be one and undivided' (4).

When entrusting to his Vicar the keys of the Kingdom of Heaven and establishing him as the rock and foundation of the Church (5), the Eternal Shepherd enjoined him 'to confirm his brethren' (6). That is to say, not only should he rule

1   Vatican Council II, Dogmatic Constitution on the Church, *Lumen Gentium*, n. 22: AAS 57, 1965, p. 26.
2.   Cfr. Vatican Council I, Dogmatic Constitution on the Church of Christ, *Pastor Aeternus:* Denziger 1821 (3050 s.)
3.   Vatican Council II, Dogmatic Constitution on the Church, *Lumen Gentium*, n. 23: AAS 57, 1965, p. 27.
4.   Vatican Council II, Dogmatic Constitution on the Church, *Lumen Gentium*, n. 18 AAS 57, 1965, p. 22.
5.   Cfr. Matt. 16, 18.
6.   Cfr. Luke, 22, 32.

and keep them one in his name, but he should also sustain and comfort them by word and in a certain sense by his presence.

We must not pass over in silence the duty We owe the Good Shepherd to seek out his sheep, who do not yet belong to this flock. Our thought and pastoral care is directed also to them so that, in accordance with the Lord's will,'there may be one flock and one Shepherd,'(7). For, indeed, 'it is through the faithful preaching of the gospel by the apostles and their successors - the bishops, with Peter's successor at their head - through their administration of the sacraments, and through their loving exercise of authority, that Jesus Christ wishes his people to increase under the influence of the Holy Spirit, and thereby he perfects his people's fellowship in unity' (8). In addition, Christ's charity spurs Us, and the mandate received from God commits Us 'to spread the faith and the sacrament of Christ' (9). It is Our duty in fact to announce to all 'incessantly Christ, who is the way, the truth and the life' (10).

The exercise of this manifold mission of Ours calls for an intense exchange of relations between Ourself and Our Brothers of the Episcopate and the local Churches entrusted to them, relations which cannot be maintained solely by correspondence but which are realised in the visits of the Bishops *ad limina apostolorum,* and by Our sending ecclesiastics who represent Us, either for the fulfilment of a special task or on a permanent basis, to the Bishops of the various nations.

7.   John, 10, 16.
8.   Vatican Council II, Decree on Ecumenism, *Unitatis Redintegratio.* n. 2: AAS 57, 1965, n. 92.
9.   Second Vatican Council II, Decree on the Church's Missionary Activity, *Ad Gentes divinitus,* n. 5: AAS 58, 1966, p. 952.
10. Vatican Council II, Declaration on the relationship of the Church to Non Christian religions, *Nostra aetate,* n. 2: AAS 58, 1966, p. 741.

It is indeed true that modern progress has providentially enabled Us to go in person even to distant continents to visit Our Sons and Brothers, giving a new expression to Our apostolic work. But this happy experience which the many and weighty commitments of the Apostolic See do not permit Us to repeat with the desired frequency, has confirmed all the more the importance of the means used by Our Predecessors which We mentioned above.

The Second Vatican Council too recognised the worth of this practice and confirmed it in its twofold aspects when it requested, on the one hand, a larger representation in the Roman Curia of persons - whether bishops, priest or laymen - coming from the various nations and, on the other hand, asked Us to clarify better the office and functions of Our Representatives (11).

Therefore, wishing to comply with the requests of the Church, We have constituted the Synod of Bishops, who in response to Our invitation come to offer Us the aid of their wise counsels and those of their Brothers of whom they are the representatives. They also come to inform us on the state and the conditions of the individual Churches (12). Similarly We wished to meet the expectations of the Council when We issued a Constitution which makes bishops from various parts of the world stable members of the Departments and Offices of Our Roman Curia (13).

Thus We now believe We are bringing to completion, in this part, the rightful expectations of Our Brothers in the Episcopate by issuing a document which concerns Our Rep-

11. Cfr. Vatican Council II, Decree on the Bishops, pastoral office in the Church, *Christus Dominus*, n. 9: AAS 58, 1966, pp. 676-677.
12. Cfr. Apostolic Letter, motu proprio, *Apostolica sollicitudo*, **AAS** 57, 1965, pp. 775-780.
13. Cfr. Apostolic Letter, motu proprio, *Pro comperto sane*, **AAS** 59, 1967, pp. 881-884.

resentatives with the local Churches and with the States in every part of the world. It is in fact obvious that along with the movement toward the centre and the heart of the Church there must be another corresponding movement, spreading from the centre to the periphery and carrying, so to speak, to each and all of the local Churches, to each and all of the pastors and the faithful, the presence and the testimony of that treasure of truth and grace of which Christ has made Us the partaker, the depository and the dispenser.

By means of Our Representatives who reside in various nations We take part in the very life of Our sons and by entering it, as it were, We get to know in the quickest and safest way their needs and their intimate aspirations.

The activity of the Pontifical Representative provides first of all valuable service to the local bishops, priests, religious and faithful, who find in him a support and a safeguard since he represents a superior authority which is an advantage for all. His mission does not put itself above the exercise of the powers of the bishops nor does it take its place nor hamper it, but respects it and even fosters and sustains it with brotherly and discreet counsel. The Holy See, in fact, has always regarded as a valid norm of government in the Church, the one which Our Predecessor Gregory the Great stated in the following words:

Si sua unicuique episcopo iurisdictio non servatur, quid aliud agitur nisi ut per nos, per quos ecclesiasticus custodiri debuit ordo, confundatur? (14). (If the jurisdiction of each individual bishop is not preserved, We who are the guardian of the ecclesiastical order would merely sow confusion).

Nevertheless, this service to the individual Churches,

14. St. Gregory the Great, Register of Letters, 11, 285

however great, does not exhaust the mission of Our Representatives. By a right inherent in Our very spiritual mission and supported by centuries-old development of historical events, We also send Our Legates to the supreme authorities of nations in which the Catholic Church is established or is in some way present.

It is indeed true that the aims of the Church and of the State are of a different order and that both are *perfect societies,* endowed, therefore, with their own means and independent in their respective spheres of action, but it is equally true that both act for the benefit of a common subject - man, who is called by God to eternal salvation and placed on earth to enable him with the help of grace, to attain it through a life of work which will give him well-being in peaceful co-existence with his fellow beings.

Hence it follows that some of the activities of the Church and of the State are in a certain sense complementary, and that the good of the individual and of the community of peoples postulates an open dialogue and a sincere understanding between the Church on the one hand and the States on the other, in order to establish, foster and strengthen relations of reciprocal understanding, mutual co-ordination and co-operation and to prevent or settle possible differences for the purpose of attaining the realisation of the great human hopes of peace among nations, of internal tranquillity and the progress of individual nations (15).

Therefore, while this dialogue aims at guaranteeing for the Church free exercise of its activity so that it may be able to fulfil the mission entrusted to it by God, it ensures the civil authority of the always peaceful and beneficial aims pursued by the Church, and offers the precious aid of its spiritual energies and of its organisation for the achievement of the common good of society. The trusting colloquy

15. Cfr. Vatican Council II, Pastoral Constitution on the Church, *Gaudium et spes,* nn. 1-3: AAS 58, 1966, pp. 1025-1027.

which thus begins when there exists between the two societies an official relationship sanctioned by the body of habits and customs collected and codified in international law makes it possible to establish a fruitful understanding and to organise an activity truly salutary for all.

The deep desire of all men of goodwill that there be a peaceful co-existence among nations, and the progress of peoples be developed, is at present expressed also through the international Organisations which, by placing their knowledge and experience and their prestige at everyone's disposal do not spare efforts in this service in favour of peace and progress.

Relationships between the Holy See and international Organisations are manifold and of a varied juridical nature. In some of them We have instituted permanent missions in order to testify to the interest of the Church in the general problems of civilised living and offer the aid of its co-operation.

Therefore, in order to place in the proper light, within the context of the Church's organs of government, the functions of Our Representatives and to give their office regulations more in keeping with the present times, 'also bearing in mind the pastoral ministry of the bishops' (16), We have decided to issue the following norms regarding the office and the functions of Pontifical Representatives, abrogating at the same time measures at present in force which may be conflicting with them.

I

1) The term, 'Pontifical Representatives' is here applied to those ecclesiastics - usually endowed with episcopal dignity - who receive from the Roman Pontiff the charge of repres-

16.   Cfr. Vatican Council II, Decree on the Bishops' pastoral office in the Church, *Christus Dominus,* n. 9: AAS 58, 1966, pp. 676-677.

enting him in a permanent way in the various nations or regions of the world.

2) They exercise the pontifical legation either only in connexion with the local Churches or jointly with the local Churches and the States and respective governments. When their legation is only to the local Churches, they are known as Apostolic Delegates. When to this legation, of a religious and ecclesial nature, there is added the diplomatic legation to States and governments, they receive the title of Nuncio, Pro-Nuncio and Internuncio, according as to whether they have the rank of 'ambassador' with or without the title of 'dean' of the diplomatic corps, or if they have the rank of 'extra-ordinary envoy and minister plenipotentiary'.

3) The Pontifical Representative in the proper sense can, owing to special circumstances of time and place, be designated by other names such as for instance 'Apostolic Delegate and Envoy of the Holy See to a government'. In addition there is the case of a Pontifical Representation being entrusted in a fixed but supplementary way to a 'Regent' or to a 'Chargé d'Affaires with credentials'.

II

1) Also representing the Holy See are those ecclesiastics and laymen who form, either as heads or members, part of a pontifical mission attached to international Organisations or take part in conferences and congresses. They have the title of Delegates or Observers according to whether or not the Holy See is a member of the international Organisation, and whether it takes part in the conference with or without the right to vote.

2) Likewise, representing the Holy See are members of the Pontifical Representation who, owing to the lack or temporary absence of the head of mission, take his place with regard to the local Churches as well as to the government with the title of 'Chargé d'Affaires ad interim'.

3) The norms contained in this document do not concern the Delegates and Observers of the Holy See, or the 'Chargé d'Affaires ad interim', unless expressly mentioned.

III

1) The Supreme Pontiff has the innate and independent right to appoint, send, transfer and recall freely his Representatives, in accordance with the norms of international law concerning the sending and the recalling of diplomatic agents.

2) The mission of the Pontifical Representative does not cease when the Apostolic See becomes vacant; it ends with the completion of his mandate, by revocation conveyed to him or renunciation accepted by the Roman Pontiff.

3) Apart from any pontifical measure to the contrary, the norm of the General Regulations of the Roman Curia which fixes cessation from office at the age of 75 applies also to the Pontifical Representative.

IV

1) The primary and specific purpose of the mission of the Pontifical Representative is to render ever closer and more operative the ties that bind the Apostolic See and the local Churches.

2) He furthermore interprets the solicitude of the Roman Pontiff for the good of the country in which he exercises his mission. In particular, he must concern himself zealously with the problems of peace, of progress and of the collaboration of the peoples in view of the spiritual, moral and material good of the entire human family.

3) Upon the Pontifical Representative also falls the duty of safeguarding, in co-operation with the Bishops, the interests of the Church and of the Holy See in his relations with the civil authorities of the country where he exercises his office.

This is also the task of those Pontifical Representatives who have no diplomatic character; they will have care, however, to entertain friendly relations with these same authorities.

4) In his capacity as envoy of the Supreme Shepherd of souls, the Pontifical Representative will promote, in accordance with the instructions he receives from the competent offices of the Holy See and in agreement with the local Bishops and particularly with the Patriarchs in Eastern territories, opportune contacts between the Catholic Church and the other Christian communities and will favour cordial relations with the non-Christian religions.

5) The manifold mission of the Pontifical Representative is pursued under the guidance and according to the instructions of the Cardinal Secretary of State and Prefect of the Council for the Public Affairs of the Church, to whom he is directly responsible for the execution of the mandate entrusted to him by the Supreme Pontiff.

V

1) The ordinary function of the Pontifical Representative is to keep the Holy See regularly and objectively informed about the conditions of the ecclesial community to which he has been sent, and about what may affect the life of the Church and the good of souls.

2) On the one hand, he makes known to the Holy See the views of the Bishops, of the Clergy, of the Religious and of the faithful of the territory where he carries out his mandate, and forwards to Rome their proposals and their requests; on the other hand, he makes himself the interpreter with those concerned of the acts, documents, information and instructions emanating from the Holy See.

3) Therefore, no Office or Department of the Curia will omit to communicate to him decisions taken, and generally will make use of his good offices to make them reach their

destination. In addition, they will ask for his opinion regarding acts and measures to be adopted in the territory in which he fulfils his mission.

VI

1) Regarding the nomination of Bishops and other Ordinaries of equal rank, it is the task of the Pontifical Representative to institute the informative canonical process on the candidates, and to forward their names to the competent Roman Departments, together with an accurate report in which he will express *coram Domino* his own opinion and choice.

2) In the exercise of this function he will:

a) avail himself freely and discreetly of the advice of ecclesiastics and also of prudent laymen who seem the most likely to provide sincere and useful information, imposing secrecy on the persons consulted out of the obvious and dutiful consideration for the active and passive subjects of the consultation as well as for the nature of this consultation;

b) proceed in accordance with the rules set by the Holy See in the matter of the selection of Bishops of the Church, while bearing in mind, in particular, the competence of the Episcopal Conferences;

c) respect the legitimate privileges granted or acquired, and any special procedure recognised by the Holy See.

3) In any case, the law now in force regarding the election of Bishops in the Eastern-rite Churches remains unchanged, as well as the practice of designating the candidates by ecclesiastical jurisdictions entrusted to Religious communities and depending on the Sacred Congregation for the Evangelisation of Peoples.

166

VII

While the faculty of the Episcopal Conference of formulating wishes and proposals regarding the establishment, the dismemberment and the suppression of diocesan ecclesiastical jurisdictions, as well as the discipline of the Eastern-rite Churches, remains unchanged, it is the task of the Pontifical Representative to promote - even on his own initiative if necessary - the study of these questions and to forward the proposals of the Episcopal Conference, together with his own opinion, to the competent Department of the Holy See.

VIII

1) In his relations with the Bishops, to whom is entrusted by divine mandate the care of souls in the individual dioceses, the Pontifical Representative has the duty to aid, counsel and lend prompt and generous support, in a spirit of brotherly collaboration, always respecting the exercise of the proper jurisdiction of the Bishops.

2) As for the Episcopal Conferences, the Pontifical Representative will always bear in mind the extreme importance of his task, and consequent need to maintain close relations with them and to offer them every possible help.

While not being a member of the Conference, he will be present at the opening session of every general assembly, and will furthermore participate in other acts of the Conference upon invitation of the Bishops themselves, or by explicit order of the Holy See.

He will also be informed, in adequate time, of the assembly's agenda and will receive copies of the transcript for his own information and send them to the Holy See.

IX

1) In view of the juridical nature of the religious comm-

unities of pontifical right and the opportuneness of strengthening their internal union and their association in the national and in the international field, the Representative of the Roman Pontiff is called to give advice and assistance to the major superiors residing in the territory of his mission, for the purpose of promoting and consolidating the Conferences of Religious Men and of Religious Women and co-ordinating their apostolic, educational and social activity, in agreement with the directive norms of the Holy See and with the local Conferences of Bishops.

2) He will therefore be present at the opening session of the Conferences of Religious Men and Religious Women and will take part in those acts which, by agreement with the major superiors, may demand his presence.

He will also be informed, in good time of the agenda of the meeting and will receive copies of the documents in order to take cognizance of them and to forward them to the Sacred Congregation concerned.

3) The opinion of the Pontifical Representative, together with that of the Bishops concerned, is necessary when a Religious congregation which has its Mother House in the territory within the competence of the Pontifical Representative, proposes to obtain the approval of the Holy See and the title of 'pontifical right'.

4) The Pontifical Representative exercises the same function referred to in paragraphs 1, 2 and 3 regarding the Secular Institutes, applying to them the pertinent items.

X

1) Relations between the Church and the State are normally fostered by the Pontifical Representative, to whom is entrusted the proper and particular charge of acting in the name of the Holy See:

    a) to promote and favour its relations with the government of the nation to which he is accredited;

b) to treat questions concerning relations between Church and State;

c) to concern himself particularly with agreements known as *modus vivendi*, with pacts and concordats, as well as with conventions referring to questions within the sphere of public law.

2) In pursuing these negotiations, it is fitting that the Pontifical Legate should seek, in the way and in the measure circumstances suggest, the opinion and the counsel of the Bishops and that he keep them informed of the development of the negotiations.

XI

1) The Pontifical Representative is charged with following accurately the work done by international Organizations when there is no Delegate or Observer of the Holy See attached to them. In addition, it is his function to:

a) inform the Holy See regularly on the activity of these Organisations:

b) facilitate, in agreement with the local Episcopate, understanding for a beneficial collaboration between the social and educational institutions of the Church and similar intergovernmental and non-governmental institutions.

c) sustain and favour the activity of international Catholic Organisations.

2) The Delegates and the Observers of the Holy See attached to International Organisations pursue their mission in consultation with the Pontifical Representative in the nation in the same territory.

XII

1) The seat of the Pontifical Legation is exempt from the jurisdiction of the local Ordinary.

2) The Pontifical Representative can grant the faculty to priests to hear confessions in the Oratory of his Legation, he can exercise his own faculties and perform acts of worship and sacred ceremonies, always in keeping, however, with rulings in force in the territory and having informed, when fitting, the ecclesiastical authority concerned.

3) He can, after notifying - when possible - the local Ordinaries, bless the people and carry out sacred functions, even those that are pontifical, in all the churches in the territory of his Legation.

4) Within the territory in which he fulfills his mission, the Pontifical Representative has the right of precedence over Bishops and Archbishops, but not over the members of the Sacred College nor Patriarchs of the Eastern-rite Churches, either in their own territory, or wherever they celebrate in their own rite.

5) The rights and the privileges inherent in the seat and in the person of the Pontifical Representative are granted in order that, by their prudent and discreet use the character of his charge may be more evident and the service he must render may be more easily carried out.

We ordain that what We have established in this letter, given *motu proprio*, be firm and effective, notwithstanding any disposition to the contrary, however worthy of very special mention.

Given at Rome, St. Peter's, on June 24th of the year 1969, the seventh of Our Pontificate.

Paulus PP. VI

BIBLIOGRAPHY

A. FONTES

ACTA APOSTOLICAE SEDIS (A.A.S.), Commentarium Officiale, Romae 1909-.

ACTA ET DECRETA *Sacrorum Conciliorum recentium*, Collectio Lacensis, t. VII, Friburgi B. 1890.

ACTA SANCTAE SEDIS (A.S.S.), 41voll., Romae 1865-1908.

CASPAR E., *Monumenta Germaniae Historica - Epistolae selectae*, Tomus II, fasc. I, Gregorii VII Registrum, lib. I-V, Berolini 1920; Tomus II, fasc. II, Gregorii VII Registrum, lib. V-IX, Berolini 1923.

CAUCHIE A. - MAERE R., *Recueil des Instructions Générales aux Nonces de Flandre (1596-1635)*, Bruxelles 1904.

CODEX IURIS CANONICI (C.I.C.) Pii X Pont. Max. iussu digestus, Benedicti Papae XV auctoritate promulgatus 1917; A.A.S. 9 (1917) II, 11-456.

COLLECTIO THESSALONICENSIS *Epistularum Romanorum Pontificum ad Vicarios per Illyricum aliosque Episcopos*, ad fidem Codicis Vat. Lat. 5751 recensuit C. SILVA-TAROUCA, Textus et Documenta - Series Theologica 23, Romae 1937.

CONCILIO VATICANO I, *Costituzione Dommatica Pastor Aeternus*, Denz.-S., nn. 3050-3075.

CONVENZIONE DI VIENNA SULLE RELAZIONI DIPLOMATICHE (18.4.1961); Pubblicazione della Societa Italiana per l'organizzazione Internazionale, Documenti XIII, Padova 1969.

CORPUS IURIS CANONICI, Editio Lipsiensis secunda post Aemilii Ludovici Richteri curas ad librorum manu scriptorum et Editionis Romanae fidem recognovit et adnotatione critica instruxit Aemilius Friedberg, 2 voll., riproduzione fotomeccanica, Graz 1959.

ENCHIRIDION SYMBOLORUM *definitionum et declarationum de rebus fidei et morum*, quod primum edidit H.Denzinger et quod funditus retractavit, auxit, notulis ornavit A.Schönmetzer, Editio XXXIV emendata, Barcinonae-Friburgi Brisgoviae-Romae-Neo-Eboraci 1967.

HARTMANN, *Gregorii I Papae Registrum Epistolarum*, Tomus I et II ....

MANSI, J., *Sacrorum Conciliorum Nova et Amplissima Collectio*, 60 voll., Paris-Leipzig 1901-1927.

MIGNE, J.P., *Patrologiae Cursus completus*, Series Graeca, Accurante J.P. Migne, 161 voll., Lutetiis Parisiorum 1857-1866.

MIGNE, J.P., *Patrologiae Cursus completus*, Series Latina, Accurante J.P. Migne, 221 voll., Lutetiis Parisiorum 1878 (Patrologiae Latinae Supplementum, Accurante Adalberto Hamman, 4 voll., Paris 1958).

PAUL VI,

– APOSTOLIC LETTER, given "Motu Proprio", for the establishment of the Synod of Bishops for the Universal Church, *Apostolica Sollicitudo* (15.9.1965), A.A.S. 57(1965), pp. 775-780; E.V., nn. 1969-2009;

– APOSTOLIC LETTER, given "Motu Proprio", for the implementation of some Decrees of the Second Vatican Council, *Ecclesiae Sanctae* (6.8.1966), A.A.S. 58 (1966), pp. 757-787; E.V., nn. 2189-2410.

– APOSTOLIC LETTER, given "Motu Proprio", on appointment of Diocesan Bishops as members of the Sacred Roman Curia Congregations, *Pro Comperto Sane* (6.8.1967), A.A.S. 59 (1967), pp. 881-884; E.V., nn. 3083-3096.

– APOSTOLIC CONSTITUTION on the Reform of the Roman Curia, *Regimini Ecclesiae Universae* (15.8.1967), A.A.S. 59 (1967), pp. 885-928; E.V., nn. 3097-3326.

– APOSTOLIC LETTER, given "Motu Proprio", on the office of Pontifical Representatives, *Sollicitudo Omnium Ecclesiarum* (24.6.1969), A.A.S. 61 (1969), pp. 473-484; E.V., nn. 3527-3588.

PIUS PP. VI, *Responsio ad Metropolitanos Moguntinum, Trevirensem, Coloniensem et Salisburgensem super Nunciaturis Apostolicis* (14.11.1789), Editio Altera, Romae 1790.

PIO XII, *Litterae Apostolicae Motu Proprio datae, De Ritibus Orientalibus, De Personis pro Ecclesiis Orientalibus, Cleri Sanctitati* (11.6.1957), A.A.S. 49 (1957), pp. 433 - 603.

REGOLAMENTO DI VIENNA *sul rango degli agenti diplomatici* (19.3.1815), in: I. CARDINALE, *Le Saint Siège et la Diplomatie*, Paris-Tournai-Rome-New York 1962, appendice VI, p. 272.

RINIERI I., *Corrispondenza inedita dei Cardinali Consalvi e Pacca nel tempo del Congresso di Vienna (1814-1815)* ricavata dall'Archivio Segreto Vaticano ed edita a cura di ..., Torino 1903.

VATICAN COUNCIL II,

– Dogmatic CONSTITUTION on the Church, *Lumen Gentium*, A.A.S. 57 (1965), pp. 5-75; E.V., nn. 284-456.

– CONSTITUTION on the Sacred Liturgy, *Sacrosanctum Concilium*, A.A.S. 56 (1964), pp. 97-138; E.V., nn. 1-244.

– Pastoral CONSTITUTION on the Church in the Modern World, *Gaudium et Spes*, A.A.S. 58 (1966), pp. 1025-1120; E.V., nn. 1319-1644.

– DECLARATION on Religious Liberty,*Dignitatis Humanae*, A.A.S. 58 (1966), pp. 929-946; E.V., nn. 1042-1086.

– DECREE on the Apostolate of Lay People, *Apostolicam Actuositatem*, A.A.S. 58 (1966), pp. 837-864; E.V., nn. 912-1041.

– DECREE on the Pastoral Office of Bishops in the Church, *Christus Dominus*, A.A.S. 58 (1966), pp. 673-701; E.V. nn . 573-701.

– DECREE on the Means of Social Communication, *Inter Mirifica*, A.A.S. 56 (1964), pp. 145-157; E.V., nn. 245-283.

– DECREE on the Ministry and Life of Priests, *Presbyterorum Ordinis*, A.A.S. 58 (1966), pp. 991-1024; E.V., nn. 1243-1318.

– DECREE on Ecumenism, *Unitatis Redintegratio*, A.A.S. 57 (1965), pp. 90-112; E.V., nn. 494-572.

B. BOOKS AND STUDIES(*)

AA. VV.,
— *La Chiesa del Vaticano II.* Studi e commenti intorno alla Costituzione dogmatica "Lumen Gentium". Opera collettiva diretta da G. Barauña, Firenze 1965.
— *La Chiesa dopo il Concilio* (3 volumi), Milano 1972. Atti del Congresso Internazionale di Diritto Canonico (Roma, 14-19 gennaio 1970).
— *La Chiesa nel mondo contemporaneo,* Torino-Leuman 1968.[2]
— *La Costituzione dogmatica sulla Chiesa,* Torino-Leuman 1968.[2]
— *La fine della Chiesa come società perfetta,* Verona, 1969.
ANZILLOTTI D., *Corso di diritto internazionale,* vol. I : Introduzione - Teorie generali, Padova 1964[4] (ristampa anastatica).
AUDISIO G., *Idea storica e razionale della diplomazia ecclesiastica,* Roma 1864.
BANDERA A., *Analogía de la Iglesia con el misterio de la Incarnación,* in "Theología Espiritual", 8 (1964) 82 -91.
— *La Iglesia misterio de comunión. En el corazón del Concilio Vaticano II,* Salamanca 1965.
BERTRAMS W., *Quaestiones fundamentales Iuris Canonici,* Roma 1969.
— *De anologia quoad structuram hierarchicam inter Ecclesiam Universalem et Ecclesiam Particularem,* in *Quaestiones fundamentales Iuris Canonici, op. cit.,* pp. 443-475 (oppure in "Periodica" 56 (1967) 267-308).
— *De constitutione Ecclesiae simul charismatica et institutionali,* in *Quaestiones fundamentales Iuris Canonici, op. cit.,* pp. 260-298 (oppure in "Periodica" 57 (1968) 281-330).

(*) Some of the Studies given in this Bibliography have not directly been used in the preparation of this book, but they were consulted - and gave some orientation - during the research time.

175

— *De Episcopis quoad universam Ecclesiam*, in *Quaestiones fundamentales Iuris Canonici, op. cit.*, pp. 409-421.

— *De natura Potestatis Supremi Ecclesiae Pastoris*, in *Quaestiones fundamentales Iuris Canonici, op. cit.*, pp. 508-527 (oppure in "Periodica" 58 (1969) I, 3-28).

— *De potestatis episcopalis exercitio personali et collegiali*, in *Quaestiones fundamentales Iuris Canonici, op. cit.*, pp. 388-408.

BERTRAMS W., *De principio subsidiaritatis in iure canonico*, in *Quaestiones fundamentales Iuris Canonici, op. cit.*, pp. 545-582 (oppure in "Periodica" 46 (1957) 3-65).

— *De relatione inter Episcopatum et Primatum*, Roma, 1963 .

— *De subiecto supremae potestatis Ecclesiae*, in "Periodica" 54 (1965) 490-499.

— *Il potere pastorale del Papa e del Collegio dei Vescovi*, Premesse e conclusioni teologico-giuridiche, Roma 1967.

— *La Collegialità Episcopale*, in *Quaestiones fundamentales Iuris Canonici, op. cit.*, pp. 351-372.

— *Vicarius Christi - Vicarii Christi*, in *Quaestiones fundamentales Iuris Canonici, op. cit.*, pp. 342-350.

BETTI U., *Relazioni tra il Papa e gli altri membri del Collegio Episcopale*, in *La Chiesa del Vaticano II, op. cit.*, pp. 761-771.

BIAUDET H., *Les Nonciatures apostoliques permanentes jusqu'en 1648*, Helsinki 1910.

CABREROS DE ANTA M., *Las relaciones de los Legados Pontificios con los Obispos*, in "Salmanticenses" 17 (1970) 2, 417-423.

CALVO OTERO J., *Relazioni moderne fra Chiesa e Stato: sintesi delle nuove impostazioni alla luce del Vaticano II e del tempo attuale. Critica di queste impostazioni*, in "Concilium" VI (1970) 8, 134-147.

CAPRILE G., *Il Concilio Vaticano II*. Cronache del Concilio Vaticano II edite da "La Civiltà Cattolica" a cura di G. Caprile, vol. III, Roma 1966.

CARDINALE I., *La missione della diplomazia pontificia*, in "Studi Cattolici" 20 (1960) 58-64; 21 (1961) 56-60; 24 (1964) 58-63.
— *Le saint Siège et la diplomatie*, Paris-Tournai-Rome-New York 1962.
— *The Holy See and the International Order*, London 1976.
CASTAÑO J.F., *La Iglesia ante la sociedad politica*, in "Angelicum" 43 (1966) 21-56.
CAVALLI F., *Il Motu Proprio "Sollicitudo omnium ecclesiarum" sull'ufficio dei Rappresentanti Pontifici*, in "La Civiltà Cattolica" 120 (1969) III, 34-43.
— *Spiritualità di fini e di metodi della diplomazia pontificia*, in "La Civiltà Cattolica" 114 (1963) 131-144.
CHEVAILLER L. - GENIN J.C., *Recherches sur les Apocristiaires - Contribution à l'histoire de la représentation pontificale (V.e-VIII.e siècle)*, in "Studi in onore di Giuseppe Grosso", Torino 1970, vol. III, pp. 359-461.
CIPROTTI P., *Funzione, figura e valore della Santa Sede*, in "Concilium" VI (1970) 8, 79-90.
CONGAR Y., *De la communion des Eglises à une Ecclésiologie de l'Eglise Universelle, dans L'Episcopat et l'Eglise Universelle*, Paris 1962, pp. 227-260.
— *L'Eglise Sacrement universel du Salut*, in "Eglise vivante" 17 (1965) 339-355.
— *L'Episcopat et l'Eglise universelle* (Unam Sanctam, 39), Paris 1963.
— *Le rôle de l'Eglise dans le monde de ce temps*, in *Vatican II. L'Eglise dans le monde de ce temps*, t. II, Paris 1967, pp. 305-327.
D'AVACK P.A., *Chiesa* (I. Cattolica, e diritto internazionale), in "Enciclopedia del diritto" 6 (1960) 961-975.
— *Il rapporto giuridico fra lo Stato della Città del Vaticano, la Santa Sede e la Chiesa Cattolica*, in *Chiesa e Stato*, Milano 1939, II, pp. 67-109.

DE ECHEVERRIA L., *Funciones de Los Legados del Romano Pontifice* (El Motu Proprio "Sollicitudo omnium Ecclesiarum"), in "Revista Española de Derecho Canónico" XXIV (1970) 573-636.

DE LA HERA A., *El pluralismo y el futuro del sistema concordatario*, in: Atti del Congresso Internazionale di Diritto Canonico (Roma, 14-19 gennaio 1970), vol. I (riservato alle "relazioni" pp. 413-431.

DEL PORTILLO A., *El laico en la Iglesia en el mundo*, in "Nuestro Tiempo" 26 (1966) 297-316.

DE LUBAC H., *Chiese particolari e Chiesa universale*, in "L'Osservatore Romano" 2-3 Nov. 1971 (traduzione del testo della prolusione svolta al Centro Culturale S. Luigi dei Francesi il 28 Ott. 1971).

DE MARCHI G., *Le Nunziature Apostoliche dal 1800 al 1956*, Roma 1957.

D'ERCOLE G., *Canones, Scriptura, Traditio*, in "Acta Conventus Internationalis Canonistarum",Romae 1970, pp. 20-38.

– *Communio - Collegialità - Primato e Sollicitudo Omnium Ecclesiarum*, Roma 1964.

DE RIEDMATTEN H., *La presenza della Santa Sede negli organismi internazionali*, in "Concilium" VI (1970) 8, 91-112.

FERNANDEZ-CONDE M., *La Diplomacia Pontificia*, Madrid 1961.

FLICK M., *La Pontificia Accademia Ecclesiastica nel rinnovamento conciliare*, in "La Civiltà Cattolica" 119 (1968) 526-534.

GALLINA E., *La Chiesa Cattolica con le organizzazioni internazionali per i diritti umani*, Città di Castello 1968.

GIANNINI A., *Il diritto di legazione ed i rapporti diplomatici della Santa Sede*, in *Il Diritto Ecclesiastico*, 1959, pp. 42-64.

GIOBBIO A., *Lezioni di Diplomazia Ecclesiastica*, vol. I, Roma 1899.

GORDON I., *De Curia Romana renovata. Renovatio "desiderata" et renovatio "facta" conferuntur*, in "Periodica" 58 (1969) I, 59-116.

GRAHAM R.A., *Vatican Diplomacy*, Princeton 1959.

GRAZIANI E., *Diplomazia Pontificia*, in "Enciclopedia del Diritto" XII (1964), 597ss.

HAMER J., *La Chiesa è una comunione*, Brescia 1964.

HERVADA J. - LOMBARDIA P., *El Derecho del Pueblo de Dios*, vol. I, Introducción - La Constitución de la Iglesia, Pamplona 1970.

JANNACCONE C., *La Personalita Giuridica Internazionale della Chiesa*, in "Il Diritto Ecclesiastico" 41 (1930) 381-443.

JOURNET CH., *Il carattere teandrico della Chiesa fonte di tensione permanente*, in *La Chiesa del Vaticano II, op. cit.*, pp. 351-362.

KARRER O., *Il principio di sussidiarietà nella Chiesa*, in *La Chiesa del Vaticano II, op. cit.*, pp. 589-615.

KARTTUNEN L., *Les nonciatures apostoliques permanentes de 1650 à 1800*, Genève 1912.

LAIOLO G., *Funzione ecclesiale delle Rappresentanze Pontificie*, in "La Scuola Cattolica" 97 (1969) 205-231.

– *I Concordati moderni. La natura giuridica internazionale dei Concordati alla luce della recente prassi diplomatica*, Brescia 1968.

– *Libertà di religione e posizione della Chiesa nel diritto dello Stato*, in *Ius Sacrum. Klaus Morsdörf zum 60. Geburtstag.* München-Paderborn-Wien 1969, pp. 767-815.

LEGRAND H.M., *Implicazioni teologiche della rivalorizzazione delle Chiese locali*, in "Concilium" VIII (1972) 1, 71-85.

– *La nature de l'Eglise particulière*, in *Vatican II* ("Unam Sanctam" 74), Paris 1969, pp. 104-124.

LE GUILLOU M.J., *Eglise et communion. Essai d'Ecclésiologie comparée*, in "Istina" 6 (1959) 33-82.

– *Le tendenze ecclesiologiche nella Chiesa Cattolica*, in *La fine della Chiesa come società perfetta*, op. cit., pp. 79-89.

LE ROY F., *La personnalité juridique du Saint-Siège et de l'Eglise catholique en droit international*, in "Année canonique" 1953, 125-137.

LOMBARDIA P., *Diritti del laico nella Chiesa*, in "Concilium" VII (1971) 8, 161-171.

– *Le droit public ecclésiastique selon Vatican II*, in "Apollinaris" 40 (1967) 59-112.

– *Los laicos*, in "Atti del Congresso Internazionale di Diritto Canonico" (Roma, 14-19 gennaio 1970), vol. I (riservato alle "Relazioni").

– *Los laicos en el Derecho de la Iglesia*, in "Ius Canonicum" VI (1966) 339-347.

MARESCA A., *La Convenzione di Vienna sulle relazioni diplomatiche*, in "La Comunità Internazionale" XVI (1961) 2, 247-273.

MARTINI A., *La diplomazia della Santa Sede e la Pontificia Accademia Ecclesiastica*, in "La Civiltà Cattolica" 102 (1951) II, 372-386.

MARTIN I., *Presenza della Chiesa presso gli Stati*, in "Concilium" VI (1970) 8, 113-123.

METZ R., *De principio subsidiaritatis in iure canonico*, in "Acta Conventus Internationalis Canonistarum", Romae 1970, pp. 297-306.

MIDALI M., *Costituzione gerarchica della Chiesa ed in modo particolare dell'Episcopato*, in *La Costituzione Dogmatica sulla Chiesa*, op. cit., pp. 525-751.

– *Il Mistero della Chiesa*, in *La Costituzione Dogmatica sulla Chiesa*, op. cit., pp. 271-367.

– *Il Popolo di Dio*, in *La Costituzione Dogmatica*, op. cit., pp. 371-519.

MÖRSDORF K., *De Sacra Potestate*, in: Apollinaris, 40 (1967), pp. 41-57.

– *L'autonomia della Chiesa locale*, in "Atti del Congresso Internazionale di Diritto Canonico" (Roma, 15-19 gennaio 1970), vol. I (riservato alle "Relazioni"), pp. 163-185.

NEUMANN J., *Neuordnung des päpstlichen Gesandtschaftswesens*, in "Orientierung" 33 (1969) 184-187.

NEUNHEUSER B., *Chiesa universale e Chiesa locale*, in *La Chiesa del Vaticano II, op. cit.*, pp. 616-642.

OLIVERO G., *La Chiesa e la Comunità internazionale*, in "Atti del Congresso Internazionale di Diritto Canonico" (Roma, 14-19 gennaio 1970), vol. I (riservato alle "Relazioni"), pp. 433-453.

ONCLIN W., *La pouvoir de L'Evêque et le principe de la Collégialité*, in "Atti del Congresso Internazionale di Diritto Canonico" (Roma, 14-19 gennaio 1970), vol. I (riservato alle "Relazioni"), pp. 135-161.

OTTAVIANI A., *Institutiones iuris publici ecclesiastici*. I : Ecclesiae constitutio socialis et potestas; II. Ecclesia et Status; editio quarta emendata et aucta adiuvante Prof. I. Damizia, Città del Vaticano 1960.

PARENTE P., *Saggio di un'ecclesiologia alla luce del Vaticano II*, Roma, 1968.

PARO G., *The Right of Papal Legation*, Washington 1947.

PARGOIRE I., *Apocrisiaire*, in "Dicionnaire d'Archéologie chrétienne et de Liturgie de F. Cabrol", t. I, 2.ième partie, Paris 1907, coll. 2537-2555.

PHILIPS G., *La Chiesa, mistero e Sacramento*, in *Teologia dopo il Vaticano II*, Brescia 1967, pp. 231-243.

– *L'Eglise et son mystère au II Concile du Vatican*, t. I-II, 1967-68, Desclée.

– *Utrum Ecclesiae particulares sint iuris divini an non*, in "Periodica" 58 (1969) I, 143-154.

PIEPER A., *Zür Enstehungsgeschichte der städigen Nuntiaturen*, Freiburg i. Br. 1894.

PUENTE EGIDO J., *La presencia de la Iglesia en las relaciones internacionales*, in "Iglesia viva" 22 (1969) 357-371.

— *Personalidad internacional de la Ciudad del Vaticano*, Madrid 1965.

RAHNER K. - RATZINGER J., *Episkopat und Primat*, Freiburg i. Br., 1961 (ed. it., *Episcopato e Primato*, Brescia 1966).

RATZINGER J., *La collegialità episcopale dal punto di vista teologico*, in *La Chiesa del Vaticano II*, op. cit., pp. 733-760.

— *Le implicazioni pastorali della dottrina della collegialità dei Vescovi*, in "Concilium" I (1965) 74-83.

RICHARD P., *Les origines des nonciatures permanentes (1450-1530)*, in "Revue d'Histoire Ecclesiastique" VIII (1906) 57-70; 317-338.

RINIERI I., *Il Congresso di Vienna e la Santa Sede*, Roma 1904.

RHODES R., *Strutture della presenza della Chiesa nel mondo contemporaneo, mediante le istituzioni proprie della Chiesa*, in "Concilium" VI (1970), 8, pp. 67-78.

RUESS K., *Die rechtliche Stellung der papstliche Legaten bis Bonifaz VIII.*, Paderborn 1912.

SABATER MARCH, *La potestad de los Legados Pontificios*, in "Estudios Franciscanos" 1963, 321-398.

SARACENI G., *"Ius publicum Ecclesiasticum" e prospettive conciliari*, in "Atti del Congresso Internazionale di Diritto Canonico" (Roma, 14-19 gennaio 1970),vol.I (riservato alle "Relazioni").

SATOW E., *A Guide to Diplomatic Practice*, New York 1962. nuova ristampa.

SMULDERS, *La Chiesa sacramento della Salvezza*, in *La Chiesa del Vaticano II*, op. cit., pp. 363-386.

SOUTO J.A., *Aspectos jurídicos de la función pastoral del Obispo diocesano*, in "Ius Canonicum" VIII (1967) 119-148.

— *Chiese particolari e Chiesa Universale*, in "Studi Cattolici" 1970, 550-554.

— *Estructura jurídica de la Iglesia particular: Presupuestos*, in "Ius Canonicum" VIII (1968) 121-202.

SPINELLI L., *La Chiesa e gli Stati alla luce del Concilio Vaticano II. Riflessioni sui principi conciliari sotto il profilo giuridico,* Modena 1969.

STAFFA D., *Le Delegazioni Apostoliche,* Roma-Parigi-Tournai-New York, 1958.

SUENENS L. J., *Le Statut la Mission du Nonce.* Interview in I.C.I., 15.5.1969, Supplément au n. 336, pp. XIII-XV.

THOMASSINUS L., *Vetus et nova Ecclesiae Disciplina circa Beneficia et Beneficiarios,* distributa in tres Partes sive Tomos, Editio prima italica, Lucae 1728.

VERMEERSCH A. - CREUSEN I., *Epitome Iuris Canonici,* t. I, Mechliniae-Romae 1963.

VERMULLEN J.M., *Le Motu Proprio "Sollicitudo Omnium Ecclesiarum",* in "Esprit et Vie" (L'Ami du clerge) 79 (1969) 611-613.

WAGNON H., *Concordats et Droit International,* Gembloux 1935.

WALF K., *Der Apostolische Pronuntius. Neue Sinngebung für einen alten Terminus technicus,* in "Archive für Katholisches Kirchenrecht" 134 (1965) 376-381.

— *Die Entwicklung des papstlichen Gesandtschaftswesens in dem Zeitabschnitt zwischen Dekretalenrecht und Wiener Kongress (1159-1815),* München 1966.

WERNZ F.X., *Ius Decretalium,* t. II, Prati 1915.

WERNZ-VIDAL, *Ius Canonicum,* t. II, Romae 1928.

ZOGHBY E., *Unità e diversità della Chiesa,* in *La Chiesa del Vaticano II, op. cit.,* pp. 522-540.

SELECTIVE INDEX

185

186

189

190